# Schooled
## *for*
# Success

"Houston has written a book that should be read by all high school students—and parents—who are looking for a productive and successful future. "Schooled for Success" is a terrific handbook for learning the basics in an easy-to-read format. A job well done!"

—Donald J. Trump

# Schooled
## *for*
# Success

*How I Plan to Graduate from*
*High School a Millionaire*

HOUSTON GUNN

iUniverse LLC
Bloomington

SCHOOLED FOR SUCCESS
HOW I PLAN TO GRADUATE FROM HIGH SCHOOL A MILLIONAIRE

iUniverse books may be ordered through booksellers or by contacting:

iUniverse
1663 Liberty Drive
Bloomington, IN 47403
www.iuniverse.com
1-800-Authors (1-800-288-4677)

ISBN: 978-1-4917-1074-6 (sc)
ISBN: 978-1-4917-1075-3 (hc)
ISBN: 978-1-4917-1076-0 (e)

Library of Congress Control Number: 2013918337

Printed in the United States of America.

iUniverse rev. date: 10/23/2013

# Contents

*Acknowledgments* . . . . . . . . . . . . . . . . . . . . . . . . . . . . *xi*

*Foreword* . . . . . . . . . . . . . . . . . . . . . . . . . . . . . . . . *xiii*

*Introduction* . . . . . . . . . . . . . . . . . . . . . . . . . . . . . . *xix*

Chapter 1    Twenty-Thousand-Foot Perspective on Life . . . . . . . . .1

Chapter 2    Back in Time . . . . . . . . . . . . . . . . . . . . . . . 19

Chapter 3    Say Cheese! . . . . . . . . . . . . . . . . . . . . . . . . 31

Chapter 4    Planting a Rich Tree . . . . . . . . . . . . . . . . . . . 45

Chapter 5    A Goal without a Date Is Just a Dream . . . . . . . . . 57

Chapter 6    More Interviews to Share and Compare . . . . . . . . . 71

Chapter 7    Music City, USA . . . . . . . . . . . . . . . . . . . . . 79

# Acknowledgments

It is amazing how a simple school assignment could turn into such a major accomplishment. I'm so glad my Advisory teacher assigned me a job-shadow project.

Thanks be to God for guiding my journey through life and watching over me.

Additionally, I would like to say a big *thank-you* to all the people listed below. You have been the biggest influences in my life and have given me the motivation for writing this book:

My mom, Michelle Gunn, for encouraging me to write this book, and for all your love and support every day.

» My dad, Greg Gunn, for your love and support.

» Grandma Linda, for the wise words of wisdom and some pretty funny stuff too.

» Lee Arnold, CEO of Private Money Exchange. Thank you for bringing me into your world for a day to see you walk in millionaire shoes. Thank you for challenging me to write this book during my job shadow day!

» Donald Trump, for the reply to my email and interview; you are a great role model for many, and I aspire to be a success in business someday.

I would also like to thank the many conference and seminar speakers, presenters, and educators that I have heard at the many events I have attended over the past four years. Your stories, personal experiences, information, and education have been great eye-openers for me in the world of business, real estate, and investing. Finally, the book would not have been such a priority to me to finish without the extra kick in the pants that so many of my teachers gave me during my freshman year of high school.

I am proud that I have been exposed to the world of business and entrepreneurs. I am thankful that my parents have felt it a priority to make the business world as important a part of my education as algebra and English class. I do need to graduate high school someday, and when I do (spring 2015), I plan to be a millionaire! So I hope you enjoy my story and my plan…

# Foreword

As I pulled open the heavy door to the conference room, I saw a young man sitting on the other side of the table. Bright red hair, brilliant sparkle in his eyes, and a charming, welcoming smile that read, "I'm excited and open for whatever life brings me next." I had just gotten my first glimpse of the remarkable Houston Gunn, the sixteen year old author of *Schooled for Success: How I plan to graduate from High School a Millionaire*.

Before I say more about Houston, let me give you a little background on myself, how I came to connect with this exceptional young man, and why I'm qualified to recognize his brilliance.

For over 25 years, I've been a performance and voice coach to some of Hollywood's top celebrities as well as developing many very talented young artists around the world. I've had the good fortune to work with such exciting talents as Drew Barrymore, Adam Levine of Maroon 5 and The Voice, Lauren Bacall, Justin Long, Jesse McCartney, and many more. I've gotten to see firsthand what makes the difference between those who aspire and those who achieve. Some of these luminaries were already successful, high achievers as young teens, much like Houston.

Before becoming a coach, I had my own career as an actor, singer, musician, and even dancer. Every once in a while I still get to do something fun on the performing end. Recently, I had the opportunity to appear on an episode of MTV's show, "Made." What a blast!

My performing career has now moved mostly to the speaker's platform and being the editor-in-chief of a digital publication, *International Speakers' Magazine*. Over the last several years, I've had the pleasure of coaching a number of top-level entrepreneurs, executives, and teams using the same high-performance principles I developed in the arts. It's been fascinating to continually discover that those very same principles apply regardless of whether someone is an elite performer in the arts or an elite performer in business.

They are principles of focus, connection, communication, mindset, passion, energy, learning to trust one's instincts, mastery of specific skill sets, and the list goes on. All of which, incidentally, I immediately recognized in Houston.

Here's how things unfolded. One day several weeks ago my friend and colleague, David Fagan, called me and asked me to come down to his office. David is a hard-charging, creative, entrepreneur who in addition to his company Icon Builder Media, recently took over as president/owner of Levine Communications Organization (LCO). LCO is one of the premier PR companies in Beverly Hills, with a 30 year track record of representing Academy Award winners, Grammy Award winners and even three Presidents.

David told me he had a young man coming in to his office for a meeting and thought it might be a good idea for me to meet him as well. That there might be some things for me to contribute to the mix. David told me this young man's name was Houston Gunn and that he had written a book which Donald Trump had endorsed. He also told me that this kid was really something.

Well obviously this did not sound uninteresting to me. Sixteen. Book written… on entrepreneurship no less. Donald Trump endorsement. I mean c'mon. "I'm in," I told David. "When do you want me there?"

As I drove into Beverly Hills, I didn't know quite what to expect. I hadn't seen any pictures. I didn't have the book to read yet. But it was all quite intriguing. All the more so because I have a great deal of experience working with extraordinary young people. I've been developing teen talent in the entertainment industry for years and have watched a number of them go on to highly successful careers. In addition to having my own coaching company, I'm also program director for the Hollywood Immersive, where we bring emerging artists from around the globe for an intense week of training and business networking in Hollywood. These hungry young people come for a program in music, acting, or hosting. And though we work with artists of any age, a great number of them are teens wanting to discover what it really takes to "make it in the big time."

So I was no stranger to the drive and passion in youth. But Houston Gunn was a complete surprise to me. And it was clear from the moment I met him that this kid was going places. Well, let me rephrase that. He had already *been* places. He was just obviously going to more of them.

When I met them, Houston and his mom, Michelle, were immediately warm and inviting. They both had that so important ability to do serious business and mean business without taking themselves too seriously. They just did what needed to be done.

Houston told me the story, quite engagingly I might add, of how he had come to write the book, of his journey as an entrepreneur since he was barely past crawling and what his plans and aspirations for the future were. I had no doubt he would achieve them.

By sixteen, Houston had already been an actor, entrepreneur, investor, and was now an author. And he showed no signs of slowing down.

During our meeting I asked him what was really important to him, what really mattered. His answer was something that deeply resonated with me. He had a burning desire to make sure other young people have the tools to be successful. Tools he didn't feel they were getting, or going to get, in school. Tools that would enable them to excel far beyond what they were currently able to conceive of. Life skills. Business skills. Outside the box thinking.

I was quite a rebel myself in school and was similarly perplexed like Houston why his classmates and those younger than him weren't being given these skills. at a time when they really needed them and had the best opportunity to learn them. Unlike Houston, who had the good sense to be born into a family with a history of entrepreneurship, I had to learn those things much later in life and not without some pretty painful tweaking of my thinking and abilities.

Houston had "nature," but he also had "nurture." His family encouraged and supported his quite evident natural talents and abilities. Make no mistake. Nurture can do a lot, but clearly Houston had the entrepreneurial "it factor." And he also had the qualities and characteristics that I saw unfailingly in those destined for great achievement.

Passion. A deep desire to inspire others. Being coachable. Seeking out the right mentors. Being unafraid to ask for what you want. Or if afraid, doing it anyway. And most importantly, a willingness to do the work, to do whatever it takes, and follow through no matter what.

Houston also burned with the right questions. Questions like, "Why aren't these important business and entrepreneurial skills being taught in our schools?" Houston Gunn wants other young people to see that there are greater possibilities for them than just finishing school, getting a job, and making do. Houston Gunn wants to be and is a true role model.

I've seen many changes in my years as an entrepreneur in the entertainment industry and now as an entrepreneur in business. We are at a time in our economic history where even artists need to be entrepreneurs to make a go of it and have a good quality of life. Every kid, and indeed every parent, who wants to better understand how to support the success of their child, needs to read Houston's book. Multiple times.

There *is* a better way. And whether you're in high school, middle school, or the parent of a student, as you read *Schooled for Success,* Houston Gunn will without question shed some light on that path. I know a star when I see one. I've worked with a fair share of them, from the film industry to the record industry, to the executive board room. And I guarantee you…Houston Gunn is on his way to being among them. I consider it a privilege and an honor to be working with a young man of his caliber.

Steven Memel

# Introduction

Hello, I am Houston Gunn, and I am an entrepreneur. In fact, I have been an entrepreneur since preschool. You might wonder how I've been an entrepreneur since preschool… you will most certainly find out as you read this book, in addition to learning how I am planning on graduating from high school a millionaire.

I am an entrepreneur extraordinaire. Currently I am a musician, real-estate investor, private money lender, and a speaker. I have also worked as a print model and an actor.

One of the reasons I became an entrepreneur is the influence of my family. My parents are entrepreneurs, my grandma was an entrepreneur, and my great-grandparents were entrepreneurs. So I guess you can say it is in my blood and runs in the family. However it does not need to run in the family. I want to spread the message to the next generation to encourage and embrace entrepreneurship as our economy and country depend on it. I am hoping this book can bring awareness to the education system to educate students and the future generation to consider entrepreneurship as an option for a career and future employment.

Other influences in my life have not only been my family, but other mentors, whether they have been in music, real estate, or entrepreneurship. Other influences I have had have been through public figures that are great role models.

I was challenged to write this in January of my freshman year of high school during my job-shadow day by a man who has been a great mentor in my life, Lee Arnold. I was just fourteen years old and worked on this book for over fourteen months. Now, as a sixteen-year-old, I want to inspire you and excite you into the world of entrepreneurship as well as investing. I hope you enjoy this book and the message it shares.

# CHAPTER 1

## Twenty-Thousand-Foot Perspective on Life

I AM SITTING BY THE window on a Horizon Airlines jet from Spokane, Washington, to Seattle, Washington. It is a very snowy evening on January 23, 2012. I am realizing that this is the day that can change my life. That fifty-minute flight only felt like five minutes, as there was so much to talk about and think about, brainstorm and dream about.

I was sitting next to my mom, who had flown with me to Spokane earlier that morning. Our day began at three forty-five in the morning with our car ride to the Sea-Tac International Airport. My Advisory class was required to do a school project for my freshman year of high school. It was job-shadow day. (Advisory class meets once a week to prepare students for their life beyond high school.)

Most of my classmates went to work with their moms, dads, family members, neighbors, or a local business person. These adults would have had to agree to let a fourteen-year-old ninth-grader come and shadow them for a day.

When I got this assignment, I was thinking very seriously about who I wanted to shadow. Who would I want to see work for the day? It is supposed to be someone in a field you might want to pursue as a career.

I could have chosen my mom; her businesses comprise a dance studio, real-estate consulting, real-estate investing, and private money lending. But I did not want to shadow her for the day because I frequently shadow her as it is and wanted to see something else.

I could have chosen my dad, who has a broad range of experience in the construction world. He is a contractor, equipment operator, and commercial truck driver. I already knew I did not want hammer swinger to be my career, and this month, he was driving semitrucks for an oil company in North Dakota—that did not interest me at all.

Then I thought, *What about Grandma Linda?* She is a successful business woman. She was an insurance agent owning her own insurance agencies for twenty-five years. She is also a developer, contractor, and currently, a real-estate investor and private money lender. *Hmmm …* that might be fun too, because Grandma Linda is always the life of the party. Something funny always happens every day when I am with her. But then I remembered she was at her Hawaii condo for the month of January, so that would not work.

My older brother, Austin, did this same project two years before. As an avid drummer and member of the high school band, he chose to job-shadow the band teacher from our middle school. I could always do something like that, but I didn't want to settle for a simple job-shadow day. I wanted something more from myself, my paper, and my assignment. I wanted more out of my future career and life.

I went into my mom's home office, where she can be found working *a lot*. That is the trait of an entrepreneur. I have witnessed that with my own eyes over the past fourteen years. Many businesses are run and business deals made via phone, Internet, Skype, and conference calls from the good old home office. I asked my mom if I could talk to her about my job-shadow project.

"Sure," she said, "what's up?"

I told her about my job-shadow project, and how I did not want to settle for someone whom I already knew what they did all day long. I wanted something different and more challenging than that.

I asked her if she would be able to email or call Lee Arnold. I have attended several of his seminars on private money lending and real-estate investing. He is a CEO of a few companies. The two I am personally familiar with are Private Money Exchange and COGO Capital. I thought this would be a long shot and he would never say yes to my request. I thought I would ask my mom to ask him for me. Maybe he would consider letting me shadow him for the day.

My mom told me she had his cell number in her phone. "Why don't I send him a quick text and see if he is even in the office on January twenty-third… then, if he is in the office and not traveling for business that day, you can text him next and ask."

As my mom sent the first text, I held my breath. With anticipation I was hoping and praying that he was going to be in the office that day. My mom's cell phone sent the text. She set the phone down on her paper-piled desk, and we waited for a minute.

Nothing…

My mom said it might take a while to get a text back. He could be on an airplane, in meetings, or on conference calls. She said she would let me know when he texted back, and then we would go from there.

I understood that I had to wait, even as hard as that was going to be. Just because I wanted to know now, I knew I had to be patient. I knew that CEOs of companies are busy people. I was sure when he could get back to her, he would. As I was walking out of my mom's home office, her phone beeped the tone of an incoming text message. I was excited, yet also scared a bit of the answer being, "No, I am not in the office that day."

She opened the text message on her phone and smiled back at me. That smile said I was going to like what I was going to read. She did not say a word; she just handed me her cell phone.

I took a deep breath and took the phone. The text said:

"I should be in the office that day as I am doing trainings at our office the weekend before. As of now, I am planning to be in the office that day. Why do you ask?"

I asked my mom to text him and ask if I could shadow him that day. She said no. I did not know how to reply, as I did not like what I just heard.

"What do you mean, *no?*" I asked, feeling my frustration build quickly.

My mom then said, "I am not going to ask him about your job-shadow day, you are."

My mom would do these things all the time to my brother and me. She would put us in the position of having to ask for what we wanted ourselves and forcing the communication to business people whether via phone or in person. At the time, it is really frustrating; however over the past two years I could see why she does it. She is pushing us to grow into confident adults and to feel comfortable asking for what we want.

So I took her phone and figured, *Well here goes nothing...* I texted the following:

"Hi, Lee, this is Houston. I am using my mom's cell phone now. I have a required school project that is a job-shadow day. We have to go to work and shadow someone all day. This person will have to do an interview with me, and I write up what I saw and experienced that day while shadowing them at their work. I am wondering if I could shadow you on January 23?"

I had my mom look over the text message before I sent it to make sure it looked okay and that what I said was fine and spelled correctly. I did not want to have my text look unprofessional. My mom told me it looked fine and to hit the send button.

I was a bit nervous, but hit the send button as she told me to do. Then we both waited for a minute for the reply to come in, and I was hoping it would come in two seconds later.

Well it took about two minutes for the reply, which felt like two hours to me. When my mom's phone did beep for that incoming text, I was super excited and hoping that the text would say yes… My mom picked up her phone and handed it to me after the beep and said, "You open it and read it, Lee is replying to you."

I opened the text message and it said, "Sure, I will put you down on my calendar that day. Have your mom get with my assistant and let us know times, after you book your flights, of arrival to the office that morning and when you will need to leave the office. Please send me any information I need to know before this job-shadow day. If there are any papers for me to fill out or anything I need to do, have your mom send them over to my assistant next week. Houston, I will see you January 23."

Wow, I got it! I get to shadow the CEO of Private Money Exchange and COGO Capital. I get to shadow someone other than my parents (no offense.) I get to shadow someone that works in a field that interests me, and I get to see what a day in Lee Arnold's office is like and a day in Lee

Arnold's shoes. He wrote a book called *Millionaire Shoes*, and I had read that book, and I wanted to see what *millionaire shoes* he walks in on a normal day at the office. I was so excited, I asked my mom to send over the job-shadow packet and papers for Mr. Arnold to review. This should tell him what to expect during the job-shadow day. My mom did that for me and confirmed with his assistant the receipt of the papers.

Then she told me we would need to coordinate getting to Coeur d'Alene, Idaho, on January 23. I asked her if we were going to drive or fly and, if we were driving, would we go over on the Sunday before the Monday job-shadow day?

She then told me that she would be out of town on business on January twenty-first and twenty-second. She would be flying back home late Sunday night, and we would need to go back to the airport about four forty-five in the morning to catch the seven o'clock flight to Spokane. We would need to rent a car and drive to their corporate office building to get there between eight thirty and nine. We could then fly back to Seattle on the last flight of the day around seven that night and be back home by eighty thirty to nine. This type of day and coordinating of travel would totally overwhelm most people, but my mom travels for business all the time, and these schedules, days, and events do not even faze her. She looked at her calendar and cleared or moved what appointments she had scheduled. I am very lucky my mom is an entrepreneur and can control her own schedule and do things like that for me and the rest of our family.

I asked her how much that would cost, and she said not to worry about it. She said she had some frequent-flyer miles that we could use. She said we would just rent a little car for the eleven hours we'd be in Spokane. Sure enough, she booked us two seats with her frequent-flyer mileage points and rented a small car. Then we planned for the day trip for my job-shadow, which would be coming up in a few weeks.

January 22, 2012, 8:00 p.m. I cannot sleep, I am so excited for my job-shadow day. I have my slacks laid out and my polo shirt for business-casual attire, as well as some black shoes instead of my usual school tennis shoes. My mom tells me to set my alarm for 3:15 a.m. so we can leave for the airport at three forty-five. This will put us at the airport about four forty-five with plenty time before our seven o'clock flight. I like to get a breakfast burrito before morning flights, from my favorite Sea-Tac Airport Mexican grill. I wanted to be sure to leave time for that too. I finally fall asleep, and my alarm goes off. Into the shower I go.

We drive to the airport right on time and park our car. We head into the terminal with my backpack, my mom's briefcase, and our boarding passes. I am really looking forward to this! We get our breakfast burritos and head to the gate. All is scheduled as planned. When we get to the gate, my mom looks across to the gate next to us and reads the board. There is another flight to Spokane as well, only leaving at six, in about fifteen minutes. It has already boarded, so there is no one standing at or around the gate. My mom tells me she will be right back and to watch her briefcase. She heads over to the gate to talk to the agent. She comes back two minutes later and says, "Grab your backpack and your burrito; we are jumping on this plane to get there one hour earlier than we had planned. They had two open seats next to each other, and they are putting us on this flight instead." WOW! My mom is always doing things like that. I am very lucky to get to see on a daily basis just how easily things like that can be done.

Now that we are on the plane, I ask her what we are going to do arriving there an hour early? She tells me that the office opens at eight o'clock, so we will just drive there, taking our time in the rental car in the snow. "That will give you extra time to get ready for your job-shadowing without rushing as well."

We landed one hour earlier, right on time, and headed off to get the rental car. I am used to riding in big cars, as my mom has always driven a Suburban or Tahoe. My dad has always driven big trucks too. Currently, he is driving a Chevy Avalanche, which is lifted really high. We walked out to this small rental car, and it was tiny! It was snowing. Thankfully, the freeways were pretty clear, but the side roads were white and covered with snow. My mom was confident and calm, though, and we made it to the corporate office right on time. We arrived and checked in, as I was eager to start my day job-shadowing. My mom was planning on working on her paperwork-filled briefcase that she had brought with her to work on that day.

As we were waiting in the lobby, I was super excited! Then the receptionist called both my mom and me back to Mr. Arnold's office.

My mom went with me to the office and then told Mr. Arnold that she was not going to tag along for the day. He then told her they had an empty desk/office all cleared off for her on the third floor. She would be welcome to work on her business there for the day. He then invited her to sit with us for the next thirty minutes or so while I did the job-shadow interview with him. We were also going to just chat about the day to come.

Mr. Arnold—or Lee, as I will refer to from now on as we are now on first-name basis—was very welcoming and excited for this day as well. He told us that over all his years of business and out of all of his employees, clients, and contacts, no one had ever asked to shadow him on the job before. He did not even know this type of thing existed with current high school assignments and requirements. He was honored that I was the first to ask to shadow him. Lee also said that he was proud of me for asking and told me what a perfect object-lesson this was: if you do not ask for what you want, you will never know if you would have or could have gotten it.

He was right, and this day proved it. If I would not have asked to shadow him, I would never have gotten the opportunity to do so. What was the worst thing that could have happened from asking? He could have said no. Where would that have gotten me and what would have happened to me then? Nothing—I would have just been back where I started from anyway. In life, you need to ask for what you want and take chances, take risks. Do not be afraid to speak up: you never know, you just might get what you want. (I will go into more detail on this way of thinking later in the book.)

## The Interview

Here is the way the morning went after we thanked and complimented each other, starting off the day.

I formally brought out my folio pad and the questions for my interview, which the school assigned. These were not my questions of choice, but a grade is a grade. If I want good grades, I must follow directions… by completing the twenty-question job-shadow packet.

I am the interviewer (HG) and Lee Arnold is the interviewee (LA).

1. **HG: Please describe your work environment. Is it outdoors or inside? Is there a dress code? Are there vehicles used? What is the physical layout?**

   LA: It is our company's office building, and we work in our offices. I work in my office or my conference room primarily. The dress code and atmosphere is business casual. Dress code for men is slacks and button shirts, and for women, it's slacks or skirts and blouses or sweaters.

2. **HG: What is a typical day at work like?**

   **LA:** I have meetings booked from 8:00 a.m. to 5:30 p.m., either in person or via phone or Internet. My days are always full of scheduled calls and appointments with either staff or clients or business contacts. I do not answer any unscheduled calls. I use e-mail very heavily and plan all my return calls one week in advance. My assistant helps schedule my calls and appointments.

3. **HG: What is the most important responsibility of your job?**

   **LA:** Managing chaos, (chuckles) and the alignments of belief and process and systems.

4. **HG: What technical skills, such as tools and computers, etc., do you need to do your job?**

   **LA:** I just need an Internet connection and a telephone.

5. **HG: What *people* skills, such as listening, teamwork, etc., do you need to do your job?**

   **LA:** It's listening that defines the heart of the challenge—Listen. Process it. Solve it.

6. **HG: What academics, such as math and writing, etc., do you need to do your job?**

   **LA:** Communication! That's it. You can hire people to do the things you don't do or you don't know.

7. **HG: How do you acquire the skills you've just identified? Education or on-the-job training, etc.?**

**LA:** Just *ask for what you want* and then tell them why they should give it to you.

[At this, I thought, Ah ha! This is what I had just realized when asking for this job-shadow day when my mom made me ask myself. I think I know how business people get what they want; they just ask.]

8. **HG: How has your job changed over the last five years—technology etc.? Has it added new ways of doing business or any new business, etc.?**

   **LA:** Five years ago, I spent little time in the office due to day-to-day dealings with real-estate development. I have gotten much better at managing my time and how I work, and now I schedule on my terms.

9. **HG: How do you think your job will change over the next ten years and why?**

   **LA:** I will make more money and do less, because I will be ten more years smarter than today. Also I love what I do.

10. **HG: How long have you held your job?**

    **LA:** Forever, it is impossible for me to get fired.

11. **HG: How did you become interested in this career?**

    **LA:** The career chose me. I knew I did not want to go to "work" for a living. Your decisions define you. I hated high school, and I did not want to spend each day for the rest of my life having someone continue to tell me what to do.

**12. HG: How did you get your job?**

**LA:** I interviewed myself; I liked what I saw, and I hired myself and made myself CEO of my company [chuckles]... Boy, these questions are really geared to interview employees not entrepreneurs. Are these your questions, Houston?

**HG:** No, these are the papers my teacher gave me for the interview questions I have to ask during the job-shadow.

**LA:** That figures. These are really questions geared to the employee mind-set. That shows you the thinking of the teachers and the schools.

**13. HG: What kind of training or education did you need after high school?**

**LA:** Dale Carnegie has a twelve-week course teaching how to be a better communicator. I would recommend it.

**14. HG: What courses did you take in high school that pertain to this position?**

**LA:** Woodshop, metal shop, volley ball, and bicycling. [I was thinking, *Really...?* and Lee must have seen it on my face, as this is what he added to reply.] The woodshop and metal shop taught me things that helped me when I was rehabbing houses to flip them. The volleyball and bicycling helped me meet girls, which helped me gain more confidence and better my communication.

**15. HG: What courses do you wish you had taken in high school?**

**LA:** The problem with high school is they do not offer any courses that teach you about how to get rich.

16. **HG: What is the most interesting thing about your job?**

    **LA:** The variety and diversity.

17. **HG: What is the salary range—low and high—for this job?**

    **LA:** It can be negative infinity to infinity and everywhere in between, because as an entrepreneur, you determine how much you make.

18. **HG: Have you always known that this was the job for you and how?**

    **LA:** No…

19. **HG: What advice would you give someone who wants a job like yours?**

    **LA:** Do not give up! Failure is sometimes necessary and encouraged… And get started *young*.

20. **HG: Do you have any other information about your job you want to share with me for this job-shadow?**

    **LA:** No, you will see plenty of it live and in-person today.

I finished my paper for the teacher for job-shadow day, and Lee said to my mom, "Why aren't we recording this? This would be a great book for Houston." We all three sat in his office and looked at each other for a moment and realized what a good idea that was. I got excited and knew then and there I wanted to make a lot of notes that day. I realized just how lucky I was to get to experience this. Lee then gave me permission to write up this interview and information in a book if I chose to do so. He said that he would also be writing another book soon, and he challenged me to get mine done first, before him. He also said that if I had a book published, he would be happy to lend me guidance and ideas on how to promote it and market it as well.

Wow! What an ending to the job-shadow interview. I knew nothing about writing a book but figured, with my mom's help and asking for what I wanted along the way, that anything is possible.

You are reading the book right now that I was given the idea to write challenged to complete during my freshman job-shadow day on January 23, 2012.

With the interview complete and the paperwork for the school and teacher out of the way, we began our job-shadow. My mom went up to the third floor and started to tackle her briefcase of paperwork for the day. She told me she would see me at five that evening, as that is when we should head back to the airport to catch our flight. She thanked Lee, and off she went. I grabbed my folio pad and began making notes. I was ready to see what Lee does in a day of wearing his *millionaire shoes*. I got to watch Lee take and make several phone calls and have meetings with several staff members individually and in a group.

I also got to sit in on a meeting with the corporate attorney and see the two of them make decisions and have discussions about business. It was great to see with my own two eyes how Private Money Exchange truly works. The company attracts lenders who are everyday people with CDs, retirement accounts, or simply cash who want to get a better rate of return on their money. The company also attracts real estate investors who are looking to borrow money for their investment properties and projects. Private Money Exchange brings the two together and creates a "win

win" for all. The borrower gets accesses to funds they need for their real estate investment, while the lender makes a much higher ROI (Return on Investment). To learn more about this please visit my website at www.privatemoneyexchange.com/mgunn or HoustonGunn.com

Lee even scheduled a working lunch for us, and we had sandwiches brought in from a local deli.

I happen to be a very picky eater. (I guess I inherited it from my dad. It drives my mom crazy, and she gets very frustrated trying to cook our family meals. Sorry, Mom.) When I heard we were having a working lunch and they were bringing food in, I got a bit nervous. I was thinking, *Uh-oh, I have to eat in front of Lee and his staff … what if I don't like whatever is coming in to the conference room to eat?* Then I began to sweat.

Then the deli tray of sandwiches came. I grabbed a turkey and cheese on white or sourdough bread, as I usually eat those… but just with mustard. These sandwiches were loaded with lettuce and tomatoes and mayonnaise as well. I simply listened in on the meetings and continued taking my notes. Then I ate the entire sandwich with everyone else—the lettuce, tomatoes, mayonnaise, and all. I was very proud of myself for not picking anything off the sandwich. I acted like all the adults and professionals in the room, who ate their entire sandwiches too. I wanted to step up to their level, so I ate it all!

Believe it or not, that was the very first thing I told my mom in the car ride back to the airport. She was so proud that I ate the mayonnaise and lettuce and tomatoes on the sandwich too. She got to remind me of the I-told-you-so moments where she had told me that I could not pick apart food and eat like a picky eater in the world. "Professionals just do not do that." She was right all along. Thanks, Mom. (Although when you make me a sandwich for my lunch at school, just add mustard please.)

## Comparisons

This day was much more educational than a normal day at school. My normal days at school consist of the following:

Wake up at five in the morning.

Leave the house by five thirty with my forty-pound backpack and money for lunch. I take both jazz band class A and class B. Jazz band A is at 5:50–6:30, and jazz band B is 6:35–7:20. Both classes are before school hours and are *zero-period* classes. I play guitar in one of the jazz bands, and bass guitar and upright bass in the other. Music is my passion. It is well worth my time, as it is the best high school band program around. Our band director expects only the best from us and has very high standards. When I leave my mom's car at five forty-five in the morning, I usually have the following packed in my backpack or in her car for the day:

» money for food

» water bottles

» golf shoes

» golf clubs

» sweatshirts

» complete change of clothes in case of rain that day. (It is the Pacific Northwest, you know.)

» music bag and folder

» guitar and bass.

This way, I am prepared for anything I need for after school, depending on the season or day of the week. This is why my mom always has to drive big vehicles!

Fall is golf season. I have golf practice or golf tournaments or marching band practice after school. Fridays have the football games; so after school, I hang out and get ready for the game about five o'clock and uniform up. The really crazy days are the days when there is golf and band both after school. On those days, I leave school at two thirty and head to the local golf course for practice until five or five-thirty, and then eat and change clothes again in the car, heading back to the high school for marching band practice from six to eight. That's when I strap those quad tams on and march around the football field for two hours. When it's all over at eight fifteen or so, then I head home to eat dinner and crash—only to wake up and do it all over again.

During the spring, I am looking forward to track and soccer. I am halfway through my freshman year, taking honors classes and participating in many activities at school. I am also attending many conferences, seminars, and business events with my mom. This causes my brother and me to miss school. She wants to bring us these events, because she feels it is just as important to be exposed to the world of Business, as well as what we are learning in school.

When Lee gave me the answer to question 15—what courses had you wished you taken in high school?—he said high school does not offer any courses that teach you to get rich. That's what my mom has been saying for years to my brother and me, which is why she felt it important to expose us to business and real estate and investing and to teach us financial literacy as well as proficiency in the standard academic subjects. I am really good at math, but I wonder every day as I am learning algebra and geometry, *When am I going to use this?* I cannot ask my parents for help with algebra and geometry homework, since they never took these classes—yet they are in business every day.

How come they do not know what $x =$ and $y =$? My mom's answer to that is, "Houston, I took Business Math and Accounting," and did not need the classes they require today to graduate. I would not and do not use them in business today. Your dad may know more about geometry, however—when he is building a house, he follows the building plans.

Why aren't the high school courses teaching me or offering courses that can benefit me more later in life? Show me how to learn more about finances, budgets, marketing, money-making, and more? I guess because the people who know these things are working out in the business world in their own private enterprises, not working for an employer like a school, teaching students. That is the difference. But that got me thinking, "Shouldn't we try to bridge that gap?"

# CHAPTER 2

## Back in Time

MIDDLE SCHOOL WAS FUN, AND I had great seventh- and eighth-grade years. I took great classes and learned so much compared to sixth grade. In addition to my classes at middle school, I got introduced by my mom to a whole new arena in business and the entrepreneurial world. She had started inviting my brother and me to attend conferences and seminars with her. They are two to four days in length and are all over the United States. These events are held on a variety of topics depending which business you are in. The events my mom was attending were on real estate and private money lending.

My first real-estate seminar was when I was twelve years old. It was put on by Trump University. I was excited to attend not only to miss a Friday of school, but also to see what these things were about and what they did all day long. Grandma Linda and my brother went too. It was a family affair that weekend. I had my notebook in hand and was anxious to see what I would see and hear and learn.

Little did I know how much this would start to make an impact and change my life. This is where I began to learn about the following:

» money

» how to make money

» how to work for money

» how to make money work for you

I like the last one the best.

Thank you, Donald Trump, for putting on that event. I am glad I attended those 3 days.

After that event, I wanted to go with my mom to other conferences around the country. She began to speak at them as well. I have only missed two events over the course of three years, and that was because I had events or tests at school that I could not miss without my grade being affected. At each event I would sit in the front row and take as many notes on my pad as I could. I would also fill up the binders that were given to you when you register. Over time, I even started getting comfortable networking with the attendees as well. One of the events included *speed networking.* This is where for the first sixty minutes, you mix and mingle and swap seats with other attendees every sixty seconds, when the music sound rings out. This results in you meeting a new person every minute.

I found this to be a great exercise and liked talking to people from all over the United States. Most all of them complimented me and said they wish they had been able to attend these types of events when they were twelve, thirteen, or fourteen years old. The nice thing was I treated them with respect and greeted them with a handshake and introduction, they treated me with respect right back.

On occasion, I have seen other older teenagers attend who might have been eighteen or nineteen years old, and they have had ear buds in their ears or around their necks and have not been tuned into the speakers or the information presented. I took special note of this and thought, *I do not want to appear uninterested to the speakers and other professionals in the room.*

Also, I wanted to make sure I was dressed appropriately, so I would wear my Polo golf shirts, nice jeans or slacks, and black dress shoes—not my school sneakers. This is important if you want people to take you seriously. You need to look the part. At first, I would have a stack of my mom's business cards in my pocket. If people asked for a card, I would hand them hers and say, "I am here with my mom." Eventually, I had my own business cards made (they had her e-mail and phone number on them, for my safety though.) People would ask for my card all the time. These events were great to go to, and after coming home from one event, I would look forward to the next one.

As a middle-school student, I enjoyed my friends and video games and sports as much as the next guy. I played golf and soccer and ran track. I also liked my classes at school. I was finding that I also really enjoyed these business events and just observing my mom and sometimes my grandma Linda when she would come along. The networking they do is amazing. By the end of a weekend event, my mom has connected with numerous speakers and exchanged contact information with them. Sometimes, we have lunch with the speakers. Her mission is not just to attend, listen, learn, and meet attendees, but to network with the speakers and the event organizers as well.

When I was in my eighth-grade year, my mom began speaking and presenting at some events. I too moved into a whole new world with her as I would sit in the back of the room and give her timing cues and point out which slide on her PowerPoint she was on and how much time was left. This is because I had her PowerPoint about memorized, and I knew when to tell her to speed up or slow down just with a *look*. I enjoyed these weekends and events: I was getting to travel and meet a lot of very professional and wealthy people.

Middle school was great! I had really good grades, and every time I missed school, whether it was for a conference or a family vacation, I would ask for my work to make up. Some teachers would give me work to do or make up, and others would not. I did not understand this. How can the teachers not know what work on Tuesday they would be giving the class on Friday or Monday? Or, if I was going to be gone for a week on a family vacation, (which we would take a few times a year), I would ask in advance for the week of work or assignments. Some teachers would give me work, but some would not. I started to become frustrated with this. I wanted to return to school caught up with my work, as I had time in planes or cars to complete it. I did not like returning to school and being behind or having a lot of missed work to do. How come the teacher would not give me the work before I left?

My mom then explained to me that if teachers were organized in their job or life or just had organizational skills, they could give the work. Organized teachers have lesson plans laid out ahead of time. If they lacked organization, then that was difficult for them to do. This is how some people are. They go day by day, week by week, and have a lack of organization. I would say I am very organized. Every time we have our cleaning ladies come to my house, other than dusting and cleaning the hardwood floor, my room is clean and picked up. At any given time, I can tell you where anything is. My brother's room is another story, so I guess that is what I compared this life lesson to, the personality traits of people. Different strokes for different folks.

This also made me look at my teachers in a different light. Instead of being the *almighty teacher*, they became just people. They are adults, moms and dads, sons and daughters, sisters and brothers, parents, spouses, and people stuck in the rat race of life.

Here, I am referencing the book *Rich Dad Poor Dad* by Robert Kiyosaki. I saw some teachers were stuck in the rat race and were just doing their jobs. Most of them did not know from one day to the next what they were going to be doing or assigning in class. The book *Rich Dad Poor Dad* was given to me on stage in a real-estate conference in Las Vegas by Lee Arnold for being recognized as being the youngest private money lender he knew. He wrote inside the front cover, "Houston, if only I had read this book at thirteen!" I started reading that book on the plane ride home from that event. I have read it two times so far and think it has good information in it for everyone to read who wants to get out of the rat race and stop living paycheck to paycheck.

I was learning as much out of school at these events as I was in school. So much so I was starting to do business myself as a lender on real estate. While my school teachers were in school teaching the lesson of the day, some days I was there and some days I was not. On the days I was not, I was at educational events learning lessons in life. I did not want to grow up and be like them. I did not want to be running the rat race of life working for money and living paycheck to paycheck. I liked being organized and scheduled. When I was in preschool and kindergarten and every day since then, my mom would have the planner filled in for the day, and in the morning, she would go over it with my brother and me. She called it her "Plan of the Day." I got in a habit of hearing that, and I liked the organization that went into that day of where we were going and what we were doing and at what times.

I am thankful my mom still uses that planner, and I hope to continue that organization in my life as an adult.

I was excited to be done with middle school finally and off to the high school where my mom, my dad, and my grandma Linda went years before me.

On my first day of school, all freshmen were invited to the gym for the "Welcome to High School" assembly led by some teachers and the principals. The leadership teacher announced for all of us freshmen "to apply ourselves in classes and have a great high-school career. Graduate with good grades. Go to a good college. Graduate with a degree and get a good *job*."

What he said next blew my mind, not just because of what was said, but how it was said—the delivery *and* the message. I was even more stunned at the response from the other freshmen in the bleachers.

The leadership teacher grabbed the microphone and chanted to us all, "If you get good grades in high school, graduate, and go on to a good college, graduate with a degree, and get a good job, most of us will make $1 million during the course of our lifetime!"

The freshmen in the bleachers in the gym went wild. It was like they all just won the LOTTO. They were cheering and screaming and acting so excited that they would get a job after college and after forty or fifty years or more make over $1 million.

*This cannot be right!* My head was spinning! So I did the math right away in my head and thought, *wait a minute…* that is, at fifty years, with retirement and investments and all, divided by $1 million. That is $20,000 per year!

And these four hundred freshmen are screaming like it is the best thing they have heard in their lives! You have got to be kidding me? I am watching the leadership teacher on the gym floor with the microphone in his hand, and he and the other teachers and principals are so excited.

They are so excited to tell us freshmen that over the course of our lifetime we can make $1 million dollars.

*Really?*

So, okay, let's do the math again. I am so bothered at this controlled chaos that has just erupted over this wonderful announcement. I feel sick. So I try to figure it out again… with forty years this time (say, age twenty-two, just out of college, to early retirement at sixty-two years old) divided into $1 million. That is $25,000 per year!

This is not looking any better, and the kids are still cheering, and it has been like twenty seconds. By now the leadership teacher on the gym floor is giving some other staff member a high five. *You have got to be kidding me—$25,000 per year is high-five material?* I am getting more confused and think this is not right.

Let's do the math again:

1 million dollars divided into 50 years- 22yrs-72yrs old=$20K per year

1 million dollars divided into 40 years 22yrs-62yrs old=$25K per year

1 million dollars divided into 30 years 22yrs-52yrs old =$33K per year

1 million dollars divided into 25 years 22yrs-47yrs old=$40K per year

Surely, this teacher must have made a mistake with his announcement as 20–40K per year is not anything to cheer about, and the students are acting like their football team has just won the state championship game.

I just watched in amazement, not liking what I heard. I was also very disappointed to watch the school staff act like that was the best news they had heard all week or all month or all year.

Is that really all there is to look forward to after getting a good education?

Every freshman in that gym was going nuts, and they were so excited about what they had just heard. It was then that I started to question what I was learning and being educated about inside of this school. Why are all these other kids, including all my friends, not upset or bothered at what was just announced?

We as the graduating class of 2015 should have been booing that announcement! *Booooooooooooooooooooooooooooo!*

In our lifetime, $1 million will not be nearly what it is worth today, with inflation. What is scary is these students do not know that. They might not have parents who know that either. I am looking around at all of these kids, and I am getting concerned. We are the future of this country, and we have got to learn more about money and be worth more than a million bucks over a lifetime!

Later that day, we got our schedules and went to our classes. I was looking forward to my geometry class, as math is my favorite subject.

Looking around at the kids in the class and listening to the teacher, I knew I was going to like this class and thrive in this environment. Over the next few days, our geometry teacher had the class doing a "get to know you" exercise. This consisted of us standing in front of the class and telling the kids and teacher three things about ourselves. Two had to be true statements and one had to be false. Then the class and the teacher had to guess which statement out of the three was the false one and which two were true. I had fun learning a little something about each of the kids in my class and was eager for my turn, as I knew exactly my true statements and my false one would be:

1.   My name is Houston Gunn.

2.   I am from Houston, Texas.

3.   I am a private money lender.

You can guess which ones were my true statements, but they could not. Born and raised in Washington, I am not from Houston, having been to the Sumner Schools from kindergarten through ninth grade, I figured a lot of the people in the class already knew that number two was false.

Yet, all the kids in the class thought my first and second statements were my true statements and that the third statement was the false one. The teacher agreed and said he thought the third statement was the false one as well.

Then I got to proudly announce the truth and explain. "I was named Houston Gunn and that was true. But I am not from Houston, Texas; I was born in Auburn, Washington, and have lived in the same house my whole life. So statement number two was false. I *am* a private money lender. Number three was true."

The kids in the class did not know what that was, and when the teacher said he had not heard of a private money lender either, I told the class and the teacher the following:

"A private money lender is someone who lends money on a real-estate investment property in first position, like a traditional bank. But these are short-term loans. These loans generate a great return for the lender. For example, the loan may be only twelve months long. The borrower may pay two to five points upfront and 10–15 percent interest on the principal loan amount, with interest-only payments each month."

I then went on to explain how the *points plus the interest* calculates the *yield* and that the *yield spread* on the deal was your *rate of return*.

I was teaching my freshman geometry class about private money lending and how to calculate a rate of return on your investment! The teacher was speechless, and I do not know if he even understood what I was explaining. The kids were looking at me with that deer-in-headlights expression on their faces, when I realized who my audience was and cut my educational presentation short. I was thinking, *Really guys? We are the accelerated math students! We are the freshmen already in geometry! How do we all know what X equals and what Y equals, but we do not know how to calculate yield?*

Then came the icing on the cake. A kid in the class said, *"Yield* is what you do in driver's ed. or when driving to let other cars go first… like when you see a yield sign."

Some of the kids chuckled, and I just said, "This is a different type of yield."

I felt so fortunate that I knew two definitions of yield. I may not drive yet, but I am fortunate that I know what both definitions of the word *yield* mean (and that I know how to do them both too).

Yield: the return on an investment. This is a term for the money you earn from interest on your dollars invested.

I came home that day from school and told my mom what had happened in the class. She was tickled pink. She said she was so proud of me. She explained that most adults do not know what a private money lender is or how private money loans work or what a private money or hard money loan even is. She explained that most adults cannot calculate the rate of return on their investments, if they even have any, and a lot of adults have not heard about the yield spread on a deal.

I was fortunate to have completed my first private money loan a few months back (April of my eighth-grade year, when I was just thirteen years old) on an investment property in Illinois, so I knew how it all worked. I was a little bothered though that more kids did not know what it was or seem to get any of it. I did not want to settle for the fact that most people go to work every day and just do their job and the duties of that job—that most adults punch the time clock and get their paychecks on Friday. Why wasn't there a math class offered at the school that could teach us finances and money management? Why can we only choose algebra, geometry, calculus, and other classes? Not all of us will use these equations in our professional lives after school, but we will very likely engage in loan transactions as borrowers even if we don't become lenders. All of us will need to manage our own money and finances. Why not start teaching financial literacy in school or how to budget, invest, and manage the money we have or will have as working adults? I am lucky and grateful that I can get this education from home, but disappointed that it is not more obtainable for everyone.

I realized that I was exposed to a broader education than most other students. I have learned many more things and have gotten to attend different events and experienced many different things. I also realized that my own household ran differently from other households. Many other moms would cook dinner and sit and watch TV or drive their kids to their activities all night. My mom would make sure we had dinner, but whatever it may have been does not mean she cooked it. She would rarely watch TV—only if we'd recorded a show she really wanted to see, and then she'd watch it later when she had a free forty minutes—and my dad shares the driving to and from any activity or event where my brother or I need to be.

My brother and I have overheard a lot of business calls in the car, and we have learned a lot from each and every one of them. As we continue to. But now, as I become more knowledgeable in her area of expertise, when she gets off a business call, I can ask her informed questions about it. She always answers my questions and explains the situation—and in so doing, teaches me a new lesson about it as well. One day, I heard my mom tell someone once that the information she was offering them cost her about

$5,000 to learn, so they needed to listen up. Since that day, I really listen up, because someday, I may need to know it as well.

This reminds me of the MasterCard commercial where the values and costs are listed for an experience, always showing the best of all experience is a feeling, which is priceless. Here is my version:

Gas for driving me everywhere:

$60

Music lesson:

$40

Overhearing my mom's business conversations on the phone in the car:

*$$ Priceless $$*

# CHAPTER 3

## Say Cheese!

SO YOU MAY BE ASKING yourself, how cheesy is this kid? How is this fourteen-year-old a private money lender? Are you thinking this is a bunch of baloney? He is just talking about what he is seeing his parents or Grandma Linda do in regard to their real-estate investing and lending. Well, I will share with you how I was able to become a private money lender at thirteen years old, and with my own money.

Now don't get me confused with a kid talking about his parent's savings account for his college education or an educational IRA account or some type of custodial account. No, I am proud to say I have been earning my own income since I was in preschool.

"Say cheese!" is the most popular phrase before taking someone's picture, right? Well I have been in front of the cameras since I was about four years old. I guess you could say I have been an entrepreneur since I was in preschool. When my brother and I were both very little, my mom got us a talent agent in Bellevue, Washington, and started taking us to auditions for print modeling, acting, television commercials, and movies around the Seattle and Portland area.

I do not really remember when I started to go to auditions. But today I see the pictures in my resume and binder, and I look about four or five years old in many of these store flyers and catalogue photos. I guess I was really lucky as the industry professionals running the photo shoots loved my bright red hair and blue eyes. I think they liked my outgoing personality as well.

There was one audition for the Bon Marché (before they turned into Macys) where I had to change into a little pair of pants and a fleece sweatshirt, and was told the photographer would snap a quick photo of what I looked like wearing that size 4 outfit. It didn't exactly go like that. This was just not a little wall to stand in front of or little room or office that I walked into. When I came out of the dressing room, I saw a full photo-shoot set with lights, lots of backdrops, cords, and *people*. I must have thought I was famous or something. The photographer started to ask if they could take my picture, and I said sure and started to do little hip-hop poses for the camera.

My mom owns a dance studio, remember? So I had just learned how to do a break-dance move called *the chair,* and I asked the photographer if he wanted to see some break-dancing. That's when I started busting a move without even any music. I was just a popping and locking and trying to spin on my back and doing the *chair.*

My mom said the photographers were cracking up, and pretty soon they were just shooting photos of me. I ate it up. After about ten to fifteen minutes, the photographers and everyone on the set had stopped whatever else they were doing and were all watching me move. I had my own audience. After about a hundred pictures, they thanked me and told me I could change into my own clothes. My mom had just been standing against the wall, being a wall flower, as mothers in that industry are supposed to do. We went into the dressing room together, and my mom gave me high fives and a big hug and said that I was really cool and that she was proud of me.

When we came out, instead of hearing the usual phrase, "Don't call us, we will call you." we were presented with a payment voucher. Then they said they'd gotten all the photos of that outfit they needed, just right then and there in the audition—no makeup, no hair, no nothing. That was the first audition I was ever paid for! I got called for direct-hire jobs after that, six or eight more times from the Bon Marché, with the same photographer.

A few months later, there I was with the fleece sweatshirt on doing my break dance moves right on the front page of the sale ads in the Sunday paper. Now, how many four-year-olds can say that? I guess I always had a great amount of self-confidence; I thought it was pretty cool to go and be photographed and get some money for it.

Every time I would get paid for a job, my mom would let me have a little bit of the money to buy a toy or something I really wanted, and the rest went into my savings account. It was a big deal to go to Toys R Us and get that twenty-five-dollar Tonka Truck, and I thought it was pretty cool.

When I started kindergarten, I had the best teacher ever! Mrs. Warwick. She worked well with my mom *and* me. She understood when I would have to leave school for auditions or photo shoots. She would even tell me on occasion when she had seen my photo in the Sunday ads in the newspaper or in the stores at the mall the weekend before. Occasionally, people from our church or other kids' parents from school or the dance studio would also talk to us about it or call my mom and say, "I saw Houston in a commercial on this channel last night" or "I went to Nordstrom's over the weekend, and Houston was in the store promo ad in a little suit eating coconut cake!" (For the record, that photo shoot was the hardest one I ever did. They really wanted me to take bites of the cake on the plate I was holding. Being the picky eater I was, cake or no cake, it had coconut on it, and I was not about to eat it. So I played with it on the fork, but it never came near my mouth.)

While I enjoyed it and liked the compliments I got—it made me feel like a little superstar—I don't usually talk about this stuff. My mom always told me if I bragged about it at school or talked about the money I had made, there was a chance my friends would not want to be friends with me any longer. She did not want kids at school or my friends to think I was getting a big head. That was good advice, as most people never knew. But when people would tell my mom and me that they saw my picture, she and I would just say thank you and then just try to change the subject or conversation. This helped me be just a normal little kid mixing in with other kids on the playground and in school.

As I got older, about seven or eight, I started asking my mom how much money each job would pay, and she would tell me the truth. Then I *really* started liking it. My parents would joke with me sometimes and say, "You just made more money today than we did!" I thought that was pretty cool, as my dad had been at work that day for eight or nine hours and my mom that night for maybe three or four, while I had just gone to Seattle for two hours that morning and then back to school. Not bad… for a second grader.

I am so glad I had this opportunity at such a young age; I do not even remember getting started in modeling and acting. My mom, being an entrepreneur, just thought differently from other parents. She didn't mind taking me away from preschool, kindergarten, and elementary school for auditions and jobs when I got them. This was not a lot; maybe after fifteen to twenty auditions of being told no, one would result in a yes. But still, while other kids were sitting in class coloring or doing PE or lunch or recess, and learning ABCs and 123s, my mom was taking me to auditions and helping me become an entrepreneur. It also built my self-confidence, as I am very comfortable in front of cameras and people and speaking on stage.

Years of dance lessons helped with that, too. My brother and I danced in a lot of state and national competitions, I was crazy enough to enter some of our own routines and choreography. The craziest routine of all was when my mom got me a little police uniform from a hotel gift shop in Las Vegas and entered me in a category called Student Chorography. I used the theme song from the TV show *COPS*, which went "Bad boys bad boys, whacha gonna do, whacha gonna do when they come for you?" I would take the stage improvising my own little hip-hop routine, doing cartwheels and break-dance moves and lip-synching the heck out of that song—like I was the best Vegas cop on the strip!

The audience would go wild. That was fun for me, and my parents thought it was great for my confidence. I never really won big, but I did get my share of awards and even prize money, but most important, it was fun.

Similarly with commercial work, I knew I would not get every job; I was told and taught that you are not going to get picked for everything, but you won't get picked at anything if you don't try out or don't show up. That makes even more sense to me now, and I am glad I learned that lesson starting from a really early age. Because it will always be true.

For example, just a few months ago I tried out for *America's Got Talent*— for the second time. I went to the audition having worked on my song for a few weeks, and strummed that guitar and sang Johnny Cash's "Folsom Prison Blues" as best I could in the time allowed—which is just a matter of seconds, not minutes. I did not hear back after the audition for the live shows, but that is okay. At least I tried out. If I never tried, I would never have an opportunity to hear back. I can chalk it up to another experience of auditioning for NBC and their camera crews and staff. I know it is still a good experience for me to grow and for my confidence to grow as well. As I walked out of the conference center that the auditions were being held in, there were kids and a few adults crying their eyes out—I am guessing because they were nervous, messed up during their audition, or simply did not get past the first cut—and I wanted to say to them, "Just try again next year or next time. It is just an audition; be proud for just trying out and giving it you're all."

I have these words of support that I use, but they could help anyone:

*You are that much of a better person after the try-out than before. Always do your best, and you will be rewarded.*

In the spring of 2009, when I was eleven years old, I got to go to an audition for Chrysler Town and Country minivans. I was in and out of the audition in about five minutes and heard the famous words as they send you out: "Thank you." Which really means "Don't call us, we'll call you."

Well, they called my agent, and I got the commercial. However, I was just hired to be an extra, which was going to be an all-day shoot with an outdoor set at a park in Portland, Oregon. that meant travel. The day of the shoot, I got to miss school, of course, and woke up at three in the morning. I jumped into my mom's Suburban, and we headed down to Portland, Oregon, where I had to be in the makeup and hair trailer by six. We arrived at 5:40, and there were a lot of people there. A lot of crew members, but even more kids. There must have been about twenty of us. I got my hair and makeup done and dressed in the outfit they wanted me to wear for the commercial, and we started to roll.

It was raining lightly, just little sprinkles. We must have run around this Town and Country minivan and jumped in it altogether thirty-five to forty times for multiple takes. But I was having lots of fun, because there was just enough moisture on the ground that every time we ran around it, the ground got muddier and muddier and more and more slippery. I like to run, and I started to think of it as a race with the other kids. I was having fun racing around the van and jumping in as fast as I could. The cameras on the booms and in the van and all around us did not bother me one bit. I was laughing and smiling and having a good old time. After what seemed like hundreds of takes with us jumping into the van, they started to do a lot of filming with us kids just running toward the camera, straight on. I thought it was good when I was moved to the front of the pack. But I had no idea how good.

When the shoot was over, about six or seven hours later, we were told we could go home. My mom and I took our voucher for the flat-fee (scale) amount that I thought I was getting for the day of being an "extra" on the commercial shoot. Then the lady running the paperwork on site that day called me and my mom into the motor home they were using for their office. My mom was handed Screen Actor's Guild (SAG) paperwork to fill out and a tax form for me to report my income.

We found out a few days later (on my twelfth birthday) that I had been upgraded to a "Principle" instead of an "Extra," as the contract shows, for that commercial. We also were told the commercial was going to be featured in the 2010 Chrysler Town and Country minivan campaign not only in the United States, but also around the world in many other countries. That's called international coverage. It's huge. Both for the reputation of an actor and for the money it pays. And it was an exciting announcement to make at my birthday dinner. My entire family was thrilled for me.

The commercial starting airing on television networks about three months later and ran for almost a year. The residual income from that one commercial is what gave me the ability to become a real-estate investor and private money lender at age thirteen. And now I can say that *I have my money working for me*. What I did for seven hours on one day gave me earnings for almost one year. But on top of that, it is what I have done with that income that continues to earn me more each day.

As my checks were coming in the mail from my talent agent, my mom was taking me to the bank with her. Every time, she would show me what I was getting paid and what we were depositing into savings accounts and CDs at the bank. I was very aware of the dollars coming in and that they were being saved for me for when I was older—so I could buy a house or car and have the accounts waiting for me as an adult. I guess the idea of purchasing a home someday seemed too far away for me; my money was just sitting in CDs and savings accounts, waiting for when I got older. That was fine when I was little, but this was now. I had been attending conferences with my mom and listening really close to speakers and educators speak on money sitting idle and money *not* working for you. I had learned too much not to speak up.

I began to question my parents, because it seemed to me that my money was not working for me. It was barely making 1 percent in the CDs at the banks! With the economy in recession, the usual inflation, and me knowing it had years and years to sit while I waited to grow up, I knew I was not making money at all. I even considered that I might be losing ground, as I was not sure it would keep up with inflation with the years to come.

I had been watching my parents invest in real estate, acquire more rentals, and fix-and-flip some properties. This was what the market in the Pacific Northwest dictated at that time. My mom would buy, my dad would fix, and they would flip. Or my mom would buy, my dad would do a little fixing up, and then they would rent them out to other families. I wanted to get my money working for me too; I wanted to buy a house... *now*, not when I was older!

So I told my parents I wanted to be a private money lender on the next house they were going to flip. I wanted five points and 15 percent interest and would loan them the money for twelve months. I would offer no prepayment penalty written in, so if my dad finished rehabbing it quickly and it sold fast, they would be able to pay me off early. Sounds a bit aggressive, huh? My mom was surprised, and I told her I had been listening to all the real-estate conferences and wanted to get my money working for me and not just sit in the bank and in the CDs making nothing. She understood and was proud that I was seeing an opportunity.

This is the most important part of my story: my parents did not come to me and ask what I wanted to do with my funds; I went to them. This was my choice to make a change and take action to get my money working for me. That was important to me and to them.

My parents had a house under contract near Pacific Lutheran University in Parkland, Washington. It was an REO (A bank owned property that the bank had to take back due to foreclosure.) and was going to be closing in about twenty days after my dad fully inspected it. I did not know this at the time. They sat me down at the kitchen table and showed me pictures and information on the MLS (Multiple Listing Service) of the property, and then they made me a different deal. The deal was as follows:

> "No, you cannot be our private money lender on the house at five points and 15 percent interest for twelve months. However … you can partner with us on this house and be a 43 percent partner on the property. You would need to bring some cash to the closing in twenty days. You would need to break a CD to make that happen, and you will have to pay some fees to the bank to do that. When the house closes at the sale to the buyer, whatever monies are made as profit, you would get 43 percent of."

My parents were not sure what the bank fees would be to break one of my CDs until they checked with the institutions. But they were offering me a 43 percent partnership (ownership) in the house, and I didn't have to do anything but park some money in it. The exit strategy was to fix and flip the property, which would take approximately three months for my dad to fix it up, and then my mom would market it and get it listed on the MLS (Multiple Listing Service). It would then take some time to find a buyer and sell it.

So I thought about that for a total of about two seconds. That sounded like a better way to make some money than cash sitting in a CD somewhere at some bank making 1 percent. I told them okay; I would be a 43 percent partner in that house.

My mom and I went to the banks the next day and found the fees that would be the lowest to break a CD out of and did it. The teller at the bank looked at me like I did not know what I was doing when I told her I was going to partner on a house. But boy I did…

My parents purchased the property in October and my dad worked on it until about February as much as he could with the bad weather and storms we had that winter. He took some time off too when we went on vacation to Mexico over Christmas break. When the house got listed on the MLS to sell, I went to see it, as I had only been there one other time before. It looked nice. My Dad did a great job rehabbing it. As I walked through, I thought to myself, *I am a partner on this property. I hope it sells quick and for a really high price!*

There was a lot of interest in the house, and my parents did get an offer. They accepted it, and then the waiting began. It took months and months for the buyers' financing to go through, but they hung on. My parents kept paying the utilities and all the holding costs every month. My dad had to go there about every ten days and mow the lawn and look over the house to make sure no one had broken in or stole anything from it (which did happen, but luckily, only once).

This seemed like a lot of time and work and a big headache. The house finally sold and the buyer moved in. When it was all said and done, I made a nice little profit on my investment. My dad was thinking that it was not really fair, as he did all the work. My mom said, in a teasing fashion, "Well the lenders or the banks make all the money and do not have to do a thing." The owner or rehabber has to do all the work. My dad did not like that reality, and this became an ah-ha moment for him, I think. He had seen costs and interest on paper before, but it was a bit different when his thirteen-year-old son could make a 43 percent of the profit in his deals. Don't get me wrong, he was supportive and still is today. It is just reality that the lenders and the banks make the money and do none of the work. I made money while going to school and playing music and sports, and he made money going to work on that house every day and getting covered in sheetrock, paint, sawdust, and who knows whatever else. While he was working hard for money, I had my money working hard for me.

After this deal, I was hooked. No more CDs for me! I am not earning 1 percent or less on my money. I would not put it in a CD for 2–4 percent, if it were out there. I had just experienced how my money worked for me and made me money, and I liked it! I talked to my mom and told her I did not want to put my money into CDs at the banks anymore. I wanted to become a private money lender. I told her that I wanted to make around 10 percent on my money and get my money working for me. I told her I had been listening at those conferences and seminars and all the classes and workshops she and I had been to. I was ready to make the next step.

I knew I would be able to lend on real-estate investors' properties and make two points upfront and 10 percent interest on my money. I knew that they would be short-term loans like six or twelve or eighteen months. I knew that my money would be secure, because it was sitting in first position on the note. As long as I was in first position, I would be protecting my investment. I figured if the borrower defaulted on any loan, I could initiate a buyout agreement and get my principal investment back or foreclose. I would just resell the property and get my money back plus more. Also, I told her that I would only place the private money loans on properties that were on a low *loan-to-value ratio* and where the borrower or owner had some *skin in the game*. What this means is that if the house were worth $100,000, I would only lend say $60,000 or $70,000; that way I had some additional room in the loan, in case I ended up owning that property someday. I could always *fire-sale i*t for $80,000. Most private money loans are done at 65 percent loan-to-value. Some hard money loans may rise to 100 percent loan to value or even 100 percent ARV (after-repair value); however those lenders are *loan-to-own* lenders.

I may have just lost some of you. If so I am sorry. That is just a small bit of information that I have learned at these seminars and conferences over the past few years.

My mom agreed to let me try my first loan, and we contacted Private Money Exchange (Lee Arnold's company). We told Lee and his lending department that I wanted to do my first loan. My mom told me she had to work with her CPA (certified public accountant) and check with her attorney about how to proceed so I would be protected in case of foreclosure, since I was a minor. She also wanted the interest payments to be reported to me for tax purposes. I have had to file tax returns for years already, so another 1099 would be okay by me.

Once she did her checking into the logistics, then I was ready to loan. I reviewed with my Mom the loans available, and we looked at a property packet for a property in Illinois. I selected that loan. It was going to be a twelve-month loan and pay me two points at the start of the loan and 10 percent interest each month. After review, I decided, along with my mom, to lend on that property and, there you have it, I became a thirteen-year-old private money lender! The loan was placed April 30, 2011—guess what happened April 20, 2012? The borrower asked for an extension for another twelve months. I readily agreed, as he had made the interest only monthly payments at 10 percent for the past year, but I asked for four points to extend. Guess what? I got them! The borrower agreed to pay me a four-point extension fee.

Here is the story with how that went:

One of the staff members in the lending department at Private Money Exchange said he was going to call the borrower and ask about a two-point extension fee to extend the loan another twelve months. I was on the phone along with my mom (in the car of course) and the loan officer, so I said through the speaker phone, "How about four points?"

The gentleman just chuckled and said well, "I will ask, but I think it will end up at two points."

I said, "Well it does not hurt to ask for four and settle for two, but if you never ask, you don't know."

I got a call about an hour later, and the lending officer said to me, "Houston, guess what? I asked for four points and the borrower said okay. You got your four points, buddy, that you asked for!"

Wow, I could not believe it! This was just another example of asking for what you want up front. What if I'd settled for the two points and never asked for four? I would have never got the four points! Just ask, and sometimes, you shall receive. So for the next twelve months of the loan, I would be getting a great return: four points paid upfront plus 10 percent interest on my money. I was happy to keep that money working for me and the investor/borrower was happy to keep his private money loan in place for his rental property that he was making money on. It is a win-win for us both!

Well, there was one person not happy and not included in the win-win situation—the manager at the local bank where I'd taken my money out of the year before. I was in the bank with my mom that May, and the manager must have remembered my CD withdrawal twelve months prior, because she asked if I was interested in taking another look at their CD rates. My mom just smiled and looked at me, waiting for me to answer.

"No, thank you," I replied. "I just reinvested the funds from that CD into another twelve-month loan where I am making four points and 10 percent interest. I do not think your current CD rates can compare to that." She was speechless, and we kindly told her bye-bye and have a great rest of her day, and my mom and I went out to the Tahoe silently. We could not wait to get in the Tahoe and have a good little chuckle and chat about that!

For any of you who may be reading this book and do not have your money working for you making a great ROI (return on investment), please take action today, and if you do not know where to start, contact me. I would be happy to help steer you in the right direction to help you gain the information you need.

You may contact me at:

www.HoustonGunn.com
Facebook: Houston Gunn
Twitter: @HoustonGunn

# CHAPTER 4

## Planting a Rich Tree

*"When you work for others, you make them rich; when
you work for yourself, you make yourself rich."*

MY GRANDMA LINDA SAYS THAT to me all the time. She also says that
to the rest of my family a lot. I like to have conversations with her about
money and business and investments. She is honest and tells me the truth
and helps me understand the business dealings that she does.

I remember when I was little, inviting her one day to a Grandparents'
Day at school. I asked her if she could get the day off and come to
my school for lunch with me for Grandparents' Day. She said to me
that she would absolutely be there, but asked me what I was talking
about?

I said the teachers told all of us kids to go home and ask our grandparents
if they could get the day off and come to the school and have lunch with

us. She said again, "Absolutely, Houston, you know I will be there, but what on earth are you talking about?"

Now, she was going to use this conversation as a learning-curve moment for me, and I did not even know it. She kept making a point of asking again and again *what was I talking about* or what was I asking her.

"Houston, why are you asking me if I can get the day off? What am I getting the day off from?" she asked again.

I did not have an answer for her at first. I started to feel confused, as I was just doing what my teachers at school had asked me to do.

"Get the day off from work, so you can come to my school for Grandparents' Day, and we are having a barbeque at school that day. My teacher said all the kids are supposed to ask their grandparents if they can get the day off and come to school."

Now this was going to get even more interesting as well as a little frustrating for me. I was thinking, *Why am I saying what the teachers want me to say, and why am I doing what the teachers want me to do, and why on earth is my grandma starting to fuss with me over this? If she does not want to come have a hamburger with me and my class, just say so.*

My grandma then asked me a question I had no answer to, and I had never ever thought about before in my entire life, until that moment. "Houston, where do I work, and who would I ask to take the day off from?" Grandma Linda asked.

I was silent. I thought for a minute, and I thought, *Well, she has a nice house and drives a nice car and goes on vacations and buys food and buys me good presents on Christmas and my birthdays, so she must work somewhere …* I kept thinking of where I had seen her at work. I kept thinking and thinking and thinking and thinking. I had been at my mom's dance studio all the time; I knew where *she* worked. I had driven in my dad's trucks to construction sites, and I knew where he worked. How come I did not know where Grandma Linda worked?

I could not find an answer to her question. I just realized that I thought I knew Grandma Linda really well, and we were really close, but I did not know where she worked. Oh no! How could this be? I knew where my dad worked and what he did. I knew where my mom worked and what she did. But I did know where my grandma worked. So I kept thinking. Well, my great-grandma lived with her, and she was always going to meetings and appointments with her. My grandma Linda was always on the phone. Even if my brother and I or my cousins and I were at her house, she would make and take a lot of calls with a lot of people and say to us to be good while she was on a phone call for some business. My mom would say the same thing to me and my brother all the time, so I never thought twice when I heard it from her. What in the heck was her business or job? What did she do? I had heard that she used to have an Insurance office but sold that business. I thought and thought, and I could not come up with an answer for her.

Well here goes! I had to tell my grandma Linda, "Grandma Linda, I do not know where you work or what your job is!"

I started to feel a little funny or embarrassed or ashamed that I did not know. She had been around me almost every day of my life, unless she was traveling or on vacation in another country or on a beach somewhere.

Grandma Linda asked me to sit down and told me that she would tell me where she worked and what her jobs were. She also told me that she would be at my school for Grandparents' Day. What she told me next I had never heard before. Though I had seen it every day, I just did not understand it.

My Grandma Linda told me that she was working every day and very hard, yet she did not go to a job or a place to work every day anymore. She said as a teenager she worked at the Dairy Freeze and loved it, as all the cute boys went there and got their burgers and ice cream cones. That is where she met my grandpa, and he drove a red Corvette. Then she said she went to college and completed one year and had a lot of fun taking classes like anthropology, psychology, bowling, and archery. When she came home from college that first year for summer break, she bought a new 1968 Camaro. She'd saved her money for a down payment on a new car working at the college lunch room all year. Her dad cosigned for her and told her if she missed one payment, the car would turn into her mother's. So she went right out to get a summer job to make the Camaro payments. She found a job in an insurance office in Tacoma, Washington. She went to work there every day for three months, and by the end of the summer, she thought she could make just as much money working in insurance as she would if she went to college the rest of the three years to get her teaching degree. She had intended to be a school teacher.

Can you imagine that? Well maybe not yet, but I am glad she quit college and was not a school teacher.

Her parents were supportive of her not returning to college, as they were both entrepreneurs. Her dad, my great-grandpa, was a contractor and built houses and duplexes. He also helped build a large addition to a church they belonged too. He donated his time and talent for almost a year, just on that project. Her mom, my great-grandma, worked alongside him every day. She was always painting, working on landscaping, or cleaning. Besides homes, they built many duplexes and rented and managed them for years. When they got closer to retirement, they started living in Hawaii for six months out of every year. When they wanted to retire, they sold all their duplexes. They sold them all on owner contracts and carried the paper for fifteen to twenty years for the new buyers. This allowed them to be the bank and make 7–8 percent interest on their money for years into retirement.

Grandma Linda said she did not return to college that fall and kept working in the insurance office for all the men who were the agents. They would arrive late for work in the morning, take long lunches, and be out of the office all afternoon saying they had appointments. Pretty soon, she was doing all the work in the office and starting to think to herself, *I can do this.*

She said in August 1972, when she was nine months pregnant with my mom, she went down to Olympia, Washington, and took the test to become a licensed insurance agent. It was the hottest day of the year, and the building had no air-conditioning. She said her long, hippie maternity dress, along with her swollen ankles clad in sandals, did not fit in with the rest of the people in the room taking the test with her. Why? Because they were all men in suits. She finished the test first and did not stick around in the heat for the results. They called her later the next week and told her that she was now a Licensed Insurance Agent. One of the first female insurance agents in Washington State. One month later, my mom was born, and Grandma Linda began selling insurance out of her home. She did that for five years while she was starting her family.

She then said she opened two offices and had very successful insurance businesses for the next twenty years. She was then divorced from my grandpa, and when she remarried her new husband, he was a real-estate broker and sold lots of real estate. He invested in real estate too.

Now I was in shock! I thought, *Grandma Linda is married too? How come I did not know who her husband was?* Did I have another grandpa? I had a lot of questions for her now.

She explained to me that she and her second husband were only married a few years and when my mom was in high school, he passed away.

When that happened, she then told me, she was running two insurance offices, but was all-of-a-sudden thrown into the real-estate world, representing him and his many deals that he had in the works at the time of his death. He was a buyer's agent, a listing agent, the broker of the office, and the investor on some projects himself. He was also partnered in a large project in our town, developing a shopping center that the superstore chain Fred Meyer was going to occupy. Then she told me that a week before he passed away, her husband introduced her to a commercial realtor named Gary.

Gary was the first person she called with real-estate questions after her husband's death. She felt like she'd been thrown into a pack of wolves. She and Gary worked together for over ten years on many real-estate ventures and development deals, and she said that he taught her so much about real estate during that time. He was like a teacher or mentor to her. Then suddenly he passed away as well, right when they were in the middle of a major deal selling property to Home Depot and Lowe's hardware stores. She then explained that she was working on that deal everyday with the developers, contractors, city planners, engineers, and many more professionals to keep it moving forward.

That is how she worked every day. From her kitchen table and with her telephone in hand. She would drive to meetings when needed, and sometimes, the business people would fly into Seattle to meet with her, on her property.

Grandma Linda told me that she did not have a boss and that she did not have to go to "work" every day at the same job and work for somebody. She did not need to ask for the day "off." If she wanted to go to her condo in Hawaii, she could just plan and take a suitcase of plans and files and go and work from there. If she wanted to go to her timeshares in Mexico, she would take her same suitcase of papers and work from there.

She then explained to me that some people work for themselves and create their own wealth and income, and it is not by reporting to someone and getting their timecard filled out and getting a paycheck every Friday. Some people work on their own investments and take risks and invest and make money that way. This is why she did not need to *get the day off* as the teachers told me to ask.

Then my grandma told me that when my mom goes to work every day, she is working for herself and does not have a boss either. Grandma Linda and my dad built all the houses on the street where we live. She asked me if I knew the building where my mom's dance studio used to be and then told me that she owned that commercial building. That is where one of her insurance offices used to be. She sold the insurance business before I was born. She asked me if I knew the building where the food bank is next door to the police station, and I said yes. She said she just sold that to the City of Bonney Lake. Then she asked me if I knew the building where my doctor's office was, and I said yes. She told me that she got the land all developed and ready for the medical facility to buy it from her and build their big building, and that the next time I go there to look right inside the front door where there is a plaque with her name on it. She gave the hospital a large donation so they could accomplish the deal, and that was her "thank-you plaque." I was in awe …

That is the first time out of many that Grandma Linda told me this line that will stay with me forever:

*When you work for others, you make them rich; when you work for yourself, you make yourself rich.*

My grandma and I talked about a lot more stuff that day and she ended up driving me to my doctor's office building, so I could walk in the front door to see the plaque with her name on it. WOW! My grandma Linda is my *hero!*

When I was putting together this book, I wanted to remember the story above exactly, so I called her on a recorded line and asked her to retell me the story you just read again and she repeated it to me just like I remembered. Only now the story is a bit longer.

She has gone on to sell a huge development to the Lowe's company. She also went on to build our city's first three-story commercial building, which was also the first building with an elevator in Bonney Lake. She has purchased and sold and done many more real-estate deals and retired again. After a year or two of reading books on the beach, she got the itch to start investing again and now is real-estate investing and private money lending and doing more business. I am so lucky. Just last month, she had a meeting in Orlando, Florida, and I got to go with her. We traveled there, and I got to sit in on these meetings about some pretty big investments and deals and situations. There were also some problems that they were meeting about finding solutions too. I got to sit in on every meeting, and on the way back, she said to me, "Houston, what you just sat in on, not very many people in their lifetime get to learn about, see, hear about, listen in on, or participate in. You are very fortunate, and I hope that you are taking this all in."

I told her that just the phone call I'd heard in the car on the way to the meeting was more educational than what I would have learned sitting in school that day. Boy was that the truth! I am so glad I have a grandma and a family that can mentor me in these ways.

Grandma Linda is my hero in more ways than one. She is the funniest person and always the life of the party or get together. She is really fun to go on vacation with also.

Some of the stuff that happens to Grandma Linda is just so silly that it is funny. Other stuff so unbelievable that when you see it or watch it or hear about it, you can almost not believe it yourself.

**Here is a paper I wrote in middle school for a "Hero" Project that I was assigned in English class. I did not get that good of a grade on it for grammar errors and organization, but that is okay. My grandma Linda has it in a frame in her kitchen at her house and my mom has it in a frame standing in a hutch in the living room at my house.**

Houston Gunn
3 -- 14 --10
Period 3

# *Grandma Linda*

My hero is my grandma because she always has a positive attitude. She also has tons of comical stories. Then she always is funny and entertaining.

One of the reasons my grandma is my hero is because she always has a positive attitude. She laughs at herself when it's funny. Whenever she does something embarrassing it seems she will laugh with everyone. She'll be happy most of the time and have a smile on her face. Also she is just fun to be around.

Another reason my grandma is my hero is that she has tons of stories. One time she runs into a junk yard dog and is like 2 inches away from it. Another time she is driving on a highway and her car stops. She ran out of gas on the highway. So she has to call the cops, and gets to ride in the cop car to a gas station. Then she has to buy a gas can, and ride back in and fill up her car. She also says every day is an adventure. She is right one time we had to ride a bus to Wisconsin from Minneapolis.

The final reason my grandma is my hero is because she's funny. She's driving to a timeshare in she goes into this zone and an alarm goes off. She is also out in a paddle boat on the lake with other people and it starts to sink. She also looking for some relatives and goes to some random house.

Heroes have the power to put a smile on your face. So does my grandma Linda that's why she's one of those heroes. She is that kind of hero because of her positive attitude, her comical stories, and is funny name entertaining. My life without grandma would be dull and boring. That's why I'm lucky that my grandma is in my life and she is my hero!

There are many, many more funny stories, and my grandma Linda and my mom and I joke that we need to write a sitcom, as Grandma Linda has so many funny things happen to her, it is funnier than anything else on TV. My mom has a pair of jeans in a grocery sack in her office and says that we need to keep those for the sitcom someday. So if you are reading this book, that needs to be my next goal. Pitch a sitcom. Does anyone know how to do that?

It's called *Grandma Linda,* and we have enough material for at least three seasons. Every time my grandma talks to me, there is something else that has just happened to her … I will give you a few hints …

   »   AM/PM

   »   Mazatlan jewelry store

   »   Denver airport

   »   junkyard dog

The list can go on and on and on…

I know I need to put a date to a goal so it is no longer just a dream, but something I can take action with by taking the steps to get it done.

So my pitch date for this sitcom goal date is… August 2014. Reader, I'm going to ask you to hold me accountable to that date or ask me via the contact information in this book, if I completed my goal. Just contact me to find out if I have pitched the sitcom yet.

www.HoustonGunn.com

We all need to date our goals and put them on paper. That first action is the biggest step toward making it happen.

Grandma Linda Sitcom
goal date
August 2014
(Date your goals!)

# CHAPTER 5

## A Goal without a Date
## Is Just a Dream

WHEN I WAS GATHERING INFORMATION for this book, interviewing people, and asking family members and business professionals questions, one thing stood out to me that I heard over and over and over and had been hearing in different ways for many years:

*Put your goal in writing and look at it every day.*

*Set your goal and put a plan in place to reach it.*

*A goal without a date is just a dream.*

I am not sure if these are quotes from someone specific or just sayings, but I like the last one the best. This is why I wanted to put the date of my sixteenth birthday to be my goal to take this book to get it published. I started it a little over a year ago, after my job-shadow day. I knew it would take some time to put all my thoughts in order and get supporting material for the entire book. So I gave myself two years. Now that the book is published, that goal is completed and off my list.

My hope is that this book helps you to think a bit differently about what you can make happen in your life and to do the following:

Set your goal. ♪ Date your goal. ♪ Take action.

To support that effort, I want you to put notes in at least four locations to remind you each day of your goals:

refrigerator door ♪ computer screen ♪ bathroom mirror ♪ car radio

Look at these notes often and read them to yourself to stay on track.

## My Current Goals

Thank you for purchasing this book, now I am one step closer to my next goals. Here is my list of remaining goals.

1. Once the book is published, take the next twelve months to market and promote it all over the world. Welcome any public speaking opportunities, media interviews, and any other forms of marketing that might arise. This will create opportunities for me to generate multiple streams of income for me and my future companies.

2. Complete driver's education and get my driver's license by 4/1/14

3. Purchase a blue Corvette by May 10, 2014, while I am still sixteen years old.

4. Get three quality songs written and record an EP by 12/1/13. (As of this writing, I have just completed the songs; now I just need to practice and work toward the recording.) Who knows, maybe

with this book, you can also purchase my music? My first track is a song titled "Let Me Be Me."

5. Grandma Linda sitcom pitched by August 2014.

6. Continue networking and getting mentors who can help lead me down the road ahead (ongoing; no end date).

My "Beyond High School Goals" have not been made yet… let's see what the next twelve months bring.

## Rules of Thumb

### Do not fear rejection.

FEAR stands for False Evidence Appearing Real.

If you think you need something from someone else to get you closer to your goal, ask for it. The very worst thing that can happen is your identified source can say no. This can happen directly—in person, in writing, or over the phone—or it can happen indirectly, when you get no reply at all.

But if you do not ask for what you want, you are saying no to yourself and will not get as close to reaching your goal. So go out there and try, ask, audition, interview, submit your work, etc. What have you got to lose? If all you get is a no, then you are in the same position that you are in right now, correct?

### Be strong and do not be afraid to take risks.

Risk can equal reward, especially in the corporate world. Now I am not talking about life-or-death risks or putting yourself or your family's safety or well-being in jeopardy. I mean, take risks by asking for what you want, trying new things—open that company, write that book, e-mail that person, audition for something, and go apply, interview, or call that contact or cold call.

A certain amount of risk is great and is what makes us grow as people.

I understand you might come from a family with a different belief system, and that is okay. For those of us who want to be entrepreneurs, we need to be able to hire some great employees someday. That is what makes our country so great! We have the freedom to be what we want to be. You might have different values, thoughts, and outlooks on life, business, school, education, children, parenting, and our country, the United States of America, and that's okay too.

I would like to thank everyone with their own individual views for reading this book; it is not my intent to change anyone, just inspire and educate whoever is interested. My intent is simply to share my story and have it heard. If one person, one day, somewhere aspires to make a goal, write it down, and take action on it, then great! If one person, one day, somewhere is inspired to become an entrepreneur, then that is even greater! We need more of you in the world!

This great country was built from entrepreneurs. As families came across on the ships to America, they did not have employment, relocation contracts for a corporation in hand with a housing allowance, benefit packages, retirement plans, or paid vacations. Those families came here on those mighty ships with a dream that they turned into goals and made real. They set up trade and commerce and offered services and assistance. They took on apprentices and mentored the younger generation.

I was very fortunate to have my mom and Grandma Linda take me on a vacation to Williamsburg, Virginia, one summer. Those towns that are set up to walk through to show you how they lived are just awesome! Every middle-school student should be able to see that! I don't think the teenagers then could even imagine what we as teenagers all have today. Cell phones, Internet, the list goes on and on. I hope that my generation can expand the mind-set of current Americans and welcome, encourage, and educate entrepreneurship once more.

Have you heard the saying, *J.O.B. stands for Just Over Broke?*

I do not want a J.O.B.

I want to find my passion and create my career.

I do not want to worry about cutbacks, layoffs, termination. If I do have to worry about those things, then I want to worry from the employer's end, not the employee's. I have watched my mom fire employees over the years and have seen how quickly their paycheck is cut off and how powerful that is. The power is in her hands, not theirs. That is a pretty great thing. Now I do not want you to think that I liked seeing that and that my mom enjoyed it one bit. However, if it has got to be done, I would rather be on the firing side than the fired side.

I want to help encourage and educate my generation towards entrepreneurship.

Why does entrepreneurship seem not encouraged with my generation in public schools today?

Where is the education for entrepreneurship, and why is it so hard to find for my generation?

*Let's all take action, find your passion and then find a way to make money at it.*

*If we can get paid for our passions, then we will never work a day in our lives.*

- » Do you like cooking? Open a restaurant or catering company.

- » Do you like baking? Open a bakery.

- » Do you like mowing the lawn and working in the yard? Open a landscaping company or offer lawn services.

- » Do you like working on cars? Open an auto repair shop.

- » Do you like painting? Open a painting company.

- » Do you like cleaning your house? Open a housecleaning service.

- » Do you like quilting? Open a quilt shop.

- » Do you like real estate? Start investing or go get your real-estate license.

- » Do you like music? Get into the music industry.

- » Do you like to write? Write a book or publish something.

For those of you who want to be doctors, dentists, engineers, attorneys, CPAs, etc., please go to college and learn your craft well.

There are so many options for us all.

My thoughts as a teenager who is now at the age to enter the workforce are a bit different. If we went into business for ourselves, just think how much that would stimulate the economy. If we are successful, then someday we will be able to hire employees and create new jobs. How great would that be? I wish that entrepreneurship was more encouraged in high school.

In writing this book, this is my thought of entering the workforce: publish a book and help spread my message to others.

My mom was listening to a DVD the other day about writing books, because this is a new arena for our entire family. We do not know anything about this. My mom said she would assist me in finding a publisher, but she had to do some research first. She had never done anything like this before and did not know where to start to guide me.

This DVD was talking about writing a book, and once you get it done, publish it and get it out there. "Good is good enough," this speaker said. So many people "get ready to get ready," being such perfectionists that they just procrastinate and never proceed to lay it all out there on the line. Why? Because they are scared of rejection. One phrase that I heard told me that my book was ready for the next step:

*Good is good enough.*

I thought, well this book has a lot of information in it; it might not be perfect, but if I do a second book, my learning curve will be much lower.

"Larry Winget says, 'My ugly book is better than the one you ain't got,'" was what the speaker said next. I was interested when I heard that and asked my mom who that was. She said, "James Malinchak." She told me that he was on *Secret Millionaire*. She went to a weekend conference in Los Angeles to learn more about books and being an author, since I was interested in this and she did not know much about this field. James Malinchak calls himself the "Big Money speaker."

I thought, *Well, I want to graduate high school a millionaire, so If he is a millionaire and was featured on ABC's* Secret Millionaire, *then he must know a little of what he is talking about.*

My mom then told me that I had met him in Las Vegas about two years ago at a conference.

"Really? Well, do you know him?" I asked, surprised.

"Not yet," she said. "However I think that when your book is done, you should send him a copy and introduce yourself to him."

So James, if—no—*when* you are reading this, thank you for those two lines, "Good is good enough," and "as Larry Winget says, 'My book is better than the one you ain't got.'" These were words I needed to hear to move forward with my goal to publish this book.

Along with my book, I had set a goal or a list of to-dos for my book and one of them was that I wanted to interview very successful people. I had a few questions that I had come up with, after a few months of putting my thoughts in order. I then created a long list of numerous people that I wanted to interview. Next, I split my list into the ones I knew and the ones I did not know or the Famous People, you might say ...

On my famous list were all kinds of people from professional athletes, Olympic athletes, NASCAR drivers, musicians, artists, actors, celebrities, talk-show hosts, politicians (including President Obama), and millionaires such as Bill Gates, Warren Buffett, and Donald Trump.

Once I finalized my list, I hit the computer and the Internet and looked up as many as I could and their contact information. I found websites, fan clubs, offices, addresses, and e-mail addresses. I then got busy and sent numerous letters out by mail and sent numerous e-mails requesting a brief, seven-question interview for my book. Some of them I heard back from, but it was with a generic reply sent by an auto responder saying something like, "We are asked for hundreds of donations and requests daily and cannot answer them all. Please go to the following website www.[you fill in the blank]." Most of my e-mails and letters went unanswered, with no reply at all.

But I was prepared for this and figured I was no further behind than before. I did get some nice fan-club mail back in return like a signed 8 x 10 photo of Mitt Romney. The signature appears to be an original with a black Sharpie… so I will keep that in my book file. Although a reply to my questions would have been really nice too.

Just when I started to think that I was only going to have interviews from business people that I already knew or my family members, the unthinkable happened.

*I got a reply …*

I got a reply from the *one* person whom I really wanted a reply from to begin with. This was the first name on my Famous People list and the first person I looked up contact information for on the Internet and the first person I e-mailed. I have already mentioned his name earlier in this book. His name is not only a name but a brand, and his name is known all over the world. I had read a few of his books, and I watch his television show since it started (as it was the one show my mom watched and scheduled her schedule around.) I had gone to a few conferences put on by his company, Trump University, over the past few years.

He is a very successful:

- » real-estate investor
- » real-estate developer
- » television personality
- » reality TV star
- » author
- » multi-millionaire
- » master negotiator and marketer
- » owner of golf courses, hotels and casinos, and more.

He replied to my request right away and gave me an interview! Talk about hitting your goals. If I would have never set a goal to write this book and then to request interviews for my book, I would have never had his interview request reply with a *yes!* If I would not have asked for an interview, I would never have gotten an interview.

This is a real-life example to set your goals and take action and do not be afraid of rejection!

Here is my interview with …

## Mr. Donald Trump

1. **What is the key to being a successful entrepreneur?**

   *You have to have passion for what you are doing; otherwise, you won't have what it takes to deal with the challenges and difficulties that will come up. After that, it's important to have focus and to keep it intact at all times. Momentum is a close third; it's absolutely necessary to keep your energy going. Passion. Focus. Momentum. Keep them in mind.*

2. **How do you think the real-estate investing market is for those who are currently taking action and for future generations as well?**

   *I've been doing well, and there are investors as well as inventory. Real estate is cyclical, so that's to be considered when investing. It will most likely always remain that way, as far as cycles go.*

3. **In your opinion, how can we encourage and awake the mind-set of the youth as well as future generations of this country into entrepreneurship?**

*A good start would be to read the book I wrote with Robert Kiyosaki, Midas Touch. It addresses many issues that would concern entrepreneurs and encourages people to learn to think along those lines. It's a different mind-set and some people are naturals, but most people can learn how to think like an entrepreneur.*

4. **Please list five advantages and disadvantages of the following: Being an entrepreneur and being employed at a job.**

*Being an entrepreneur:*

1. *You're in charge./You have more responsibility.*

2. *The challenges are there./Failure is a possibility.*

3. *The excitement is there./The anxiety is there.*

4. *Independence feels great./It's not a group effort.*

5. *The achievement is yours./There's no one else to blame.*

6. *\*It's great to be creating jobs.*

*Being employed at a job:*

1. *Security/Not as much freedom*

2. *Group effort/Can be conflicts*

3. *Challenge with your position/Difficulties*

4. *Learning something new/Struggling with the "new"*

5. *Exposure to a variety of people/People skills put to the test*

5. **How do you feel about the unemployment rates in our country, and how would you change the mind-sets of those collecting it to an entrepreneurial mind-set?**

*It's a big problem and has been for too long. I would hope people would read Midas Touch and start revamping their approach to earning a living. It takes more effort, but it is worth it, and it's a great feeling to be creating jobs for people. We need entrepreneurs.*

6. **As successful as you are with your company, what would you say is the greatest asset to managing a company?**

*Passion. Focus. Momentum. I've mentioned that before, but that's what it takes. You also have to have a great team to work with—people with the same work ethic. I work quickly, and I need people who can keep up—so that they are an asset to me and the company. Every company has its own ethos. The Trump brand represents the gold standard, and that's what is expected. It helps to have a standard that is very clear.*

7. **If you could go back to being fourteen years old again, what would you do differently?**

*I wouldn't do anything differently. I am very happy—love my family and my work, and so I have no reason to change anything—perhaps except the way I comb my hair.*

*Donald J. Trump*

I think the last line is the best! "Learn how to comb his hair." That is a perfect marketing message right there. He is famous for his hair.

Thank you, Mr. Donald Trump for the interview for my book. I sent out over a hundred requests to famous and successful people, and you were my one and only reply. This is the best interview, I could have gotten with the topic of my book.

Thank you for taking the time out of your busy schedule to comment on entrepreneurship and the opportunities ahead. Thank you for your opinion and encouragement of our youth today!

When this gets published, I will be coming by your office building in New York to deliver you a personal signed copy of this book. (And of course a great big Thank-You Card!)

# CHAPTER 6

## More Interviews to Share and Compare

I HAVE A FEW OTHER interesting interviews to share and compare with the same seven questions that I asked Donald Trump. I hope you find these as interesting as I do.

### Jim Lipscomb

I interviewed Jim Lipscomb, who is a retired commercial airline pilot and real-estate investor and hard money lender in Salt Lake City.

I met him at a conference in April 2012; he was seated near us, so we got to visiting during the event. On a break on the third day, I asked him if I could interview him for my book, and he agreed. I hope you enjoy is his interview.

1. **What is the key to being a successful entrepreneur?**

   *Unshakeable confidence in yourself.*

2. **How do you think the real-estate investment market is for those who are currently taking action and for future generations as well?**

   *Wonderful question; and yes, there will always be a spread between wholesale and retail real-estate transactions.*

3. **In your opinion, how can we encourage and awake the mindset of the youth as well as future generations of the country into entrepreneurship?**

   *Most youth have never been held accountable for their actions. They always want to blame someone else; they will say its someone else's fault or have an excuse. They do not have personal accountability. Hesitation is a fear, fear of failing. Most have never left their comfort zone. No one can give you self-confidence but you. Leaders are the people who are not lazy to work, are very honest with themselves and others, and would never steal.*

4. **Please list five advantages and five disadvantages of being an entrepreneur and being employed at a job.**

   *Entrepreneur advantages:*

   1. *Passion takes you to the field you want to work in.*
   2. *If you have passion, you will always do well.*
   3. *You never have a job, just challenges.*

*Entrepreneur disadvantages:*

1. *There is no one to help you.*

2. *The reality is you may fail multiple times.*

3. *There is no such thing as a forty-hour work week.*

*Being employed at a job advantages:*

1. *You get predetermined rewards such as pay, benefits, and bonuses.*

2. *You work under predetermined expectations to keep your job.*

3. *Predetermined effort.*

4. *Security.*

*Being employed at a job disadvantages:*

1. *Lack of fulfillment.*

2. *Lack of advancement.*

3. *Lack of recognition.*

5. **How do you feel about the unemployment rates in our country, and how would you change the mind-sets of those collecting it to an entrepreneurial mind-set?**

   *Unemployment is high, but if anyone wants a job, they can find one. We can try to change minds to accept change instead of fear change. Most people could be an entrepreneur. It is not a trait or a talent. But for most, the fear of failure is greater than the happiness of success.*

6. **As successful as you are, what would you say is the greatest asset to managing a business or your real-estate investing?**

   *Successful managers lead with vision and can communicate their vision.*

7. **If you could go back to being fourteen years old again, what would you do differently?**

*I have had a successful life. I would only make small changes to remove hurt and sorrow, but other than that, I would not change much.*

*Please add these quotes:*

> *If you always do what you've always done, you will always have what you already have got.*

> *If you love what you do, then you do not have a job.*

Thank you, Jim, for the great interview, and I enjoyed meeting you in Seattle!

## Grandma Linda

Next I want to share the same interview questions with Grandma Linda, which I conducted by phone when she was in Hawaii.

1. **What is the key to being a successful entrepreneur?**

*Hard work and 24-7*

2. **How do you think the real-estate investing market is for those who are currently taking action and for future generations as well?**

*I think it is medium to poor right now compared to what I have seen in my lifetime. In the past, you were able to buy a piece of property and it grew with appreciation and in value over years. Now when you buy a piece of property, it may go up, it may stay the same, or it may go down. Many families have seen their values go down.*

3.  In your opinion, how can we encourage and awake the mind-set of the youth as well as future generations of this country into entrepreneurship?

    *Entrepreneurship needs to be encouraged in school, and Houston, I am so proud of you for writing this book. Young people need to start being educated and encouraged early and taught about entrepreneurship. By the time they are eighteen, nineteen, or twenty, for most, it is too late, and they are heading already in the direction their head is telling them to go. We need to have more tools for entrepreneurs, and when we educate, we need to teach about the positives and also the negatives.*

4.  Please list five advantages and disadvantages of being an entrepreneur and being employed at a job.

    *Entrepreneur advantages:*

    1.  *You are your own boss.*
    2.  *The more hard work you put in, the more your business should grow.*
    3.  *You can run your business in one direction, and if it is not working, you can change it and take it into another direction and do something differently.*
    4.  *You can pick your hours you want to work.*
    5.  *You can choose to work by yourself or with a partner or employees.*

    *Entrepreneur disadvantages:*

    1.  *The only one who is going to give you a paycheck is yourself.*
    2.  *You don't get to "clock in" and suddenly get paid to work.*
    3.  *You don't get benefits, and if you want them, you have to pay for them.*
    4.  *You have to work hard to find customers, and once you find them, you have to keep them happy.*
    5.  *It is pure risk.*

*Being employed at a job advantages:*

1. *You get to arrive and leave at certain times.*

2. *When you leave work, you do not have to do anything work-related or even think about it until you return next time.*

3. *You get your regular, scheduled paycheck.*

4. *You get benefits.*

5. *You get paid days off and paid vacations.*

*Being employed at a job disadvantages:*

1. *You will make the same amount of money every day and every hour unless you get a raise.*

2. *You have to answer to your boss.*

3. *You are given a list of tasks to do, and you must complete the list on time.*

4. *Your vacations and time off may not be at the time you want off.*

5. *There is a ceiling to how much you can make at every job.*

5. **How do you feel about the unemployment rates in our country, and how would you change the mind-sets of those collecting it to an entrepreneurial mind set?**

   *It needs to start to be taught young. Most adults are fearful of not having a job, as they already have the employee mind-set—and that is very difficult to change.*

6. **As successful as you are with your company, what would you say is the greatest asset to managing the company?**

   *The attitude that the sky is the limit, depending on how hard you want to work.*

7. **If you could go back to being fourteen years old again, what would you do differently?**

*Nothing! I would not change a thing. Houston, I want to encourage you to write your book and then don't stop at just that one book. Write more. I wish you all the luck in the world with your book and with your music and the career that you want to have in the music industry—and that I think you are going to have. You are doing great things, and you will be very successful.*

Thank you Grandma Linda for the interview. You are my *hero!*

I had lunch with the Mayor of Sumner, Washington, while writing this book. He told me when I had the book done and published, to bring a copy by City Hall. And then he said, "I do not know if we have ever done anything like this before, but maybe we need to do a parade or book signing or something in front of your school."

"Thank you, I would love a parade or book signing in front of Sumner High School!"

Thank you, Mr. Mayor, for lunch. I look forward to bringing a copy of my book to City Hall and hopefully your offer of a parade or a book signing or something like that still stands. However, it can be in front of the high school.

Oh, there's one little problem ... my school is now 2,500 miles away! I do not go to school there anymore.

# CHAPTER 7

## Music City, USA

So MY FRESHMAN YEAR OF high school was turning out to be the biggest year of my life! I was experiencing, learning, and being exposed to so much. I had my book started and was setting goals. What I did not know was that my mom had set some goals for herself and our family too. She dated these goals. They were *really big goals!* The kind of goals that change your life—literally!

The nice thing about goals is that once you date them, they are still just a goal. They can change, and you can adjust the date if you need to. My parents had a goal. They were going to go to Nashville, Tennessee, the first week of January 2011 to start to look at properties and possibly buy a house there. At that time, my brother and I both balked at that idea, as we had our friends at school, you know … Nonetheless, they were planning the trip, and their hotel and airfare was booked. They were leaving on January third, the day that we went back to school from Christmas break; my grandma Linda would be staying with my brother and me.

Well, on January 1, 2011 at 1:11 p.m., their Nashville trip was put on the back burner for quite some time.

We were all watching one of the New Year's Day football games on TV, and my mom was just starting to take decorations off our Christmas tree, when the phone rang. It was an alarm monitoring company for my mom's dance studio business and one of the commercial buildings that my parents owned. They had an alarm in progress. It was icy and still a bit snowy out, as we had very cold temperatures that entire week. My parents, my brother and I, and my friend who was hanging out with us all threw on our shoes and ran out the door, jumped in the car and went to see what was happening.

We arrived to see a four-thousand-square-foot building, which was supposed to be a dance studio, that looked like an indoor water park. We waded in the water as we came in the front door. Water was spraying from the ceiling in a few spots. There were frozen and broken pipes in the ceiling of the building.

All my dad said when he looked at my mom was "This is really bad," and then he went to work shutting off the water and doing what he could.

This happened on 1-1-11 at 1:11 p.m., and my mom said that must be a sign, and God does not want us to go to Nashville, on this trip, at this time. This resulted in the canceling of their trip, and I did not see my dad until Valentine's Day, as he was working at that building from about six in the morning to eleven at night every day. My mom's business operated out of a local community hall, a middle school cafeteria, and the city senior center. The whole idea of moving to Nashville for our family was on hold for now.

One year later, my mom started talking to us about moving to Nashville again. We had been there several times before on vacation, and she liked the opportunity that it had for my brother and me furthering our music education with access to Music City, USA.

If we were interested, she would like to go look at houses around Nashville. She liked the people, the politics, the cost of living, and the idea of doing business there as well. Also, she liked the idea of living in the "belt buckle of the Bible belt." I was now halfway through my freshman year and just starting my book. A lot had changed for me since my job-shadow day that year, and my outlook on life had started to look a bit different too. My brother was instantly sold on the idea of moving and said that he always wanted to be a country boy and wanted to start hunting. He asked if we could get a house with lots of room, so he could ride quads and his motorcycle around his house and not have to load it up in his truck and drive an hour away to ride, as he had to do in Washington. We have had the police called to our house many times for him just starting his bike in the driveway while cleaning it. Those darn city noise ordinances…

I was the one really excited, as I could really further my music in Music City, USA. I told her that I wanted to go with her and check everything out. So my mom said when she planned a trip to Nashville later that year, she would plan to take me so I could fully check it out with her and see the schools and the area. Living there would be much different from vacationing there. I was fine with that, because I knew nothing would happen until I went to Nashville with her and because I would be part of the process and the investigation of this new venture.

I did not know that my mom had a date for her goal of June 2013 and was positioning and planning to sell a business and two properties in the few months before school was out. She had set a goal a few years back for herself to move her family there before my brother and I left home, as she knew if we left home before we relocated, we would never really call Tennessee home. She also knew it would be easy for us to transition into that area at our current ages. It would be easy to meet kids at school and other places.

I liked school and always did well in school. I got really good grades—that is, until ninth-grade Honors English. I am not proud to say that I got an F in that class. I flunked by one and a half points. Luckily, I get to take ninth-grade English again next year in Tennessee, along with my eleventh-grade English class. I'd like to share an example of what led me to fail that class.

We had an assignment to do a research paper of a thousand words on the topic of our choice. What I am about to share with you all is an example of what I know now is a life lesson of standing up for yourself and what you believe in and feel is right. I learned the hard way, this teacher did not like to feel challenged, and when students want to do what they feel is right, the grades sometimes reflect the teacher's displeasure more than the quality of the work. (My brother has even worse examples of this. No wonder my mom wanted to move to Nashville.)

I was excited to do this research paper, since I was starting to write my own book already and had chosen my topic of first-trust deed lending. My thought was that I would do the research paper and then make it part of my book. That was going to be perfect!

Then it was time to turn in our topics of choice.

(Hold on one minute if you are reading this and make sure you are sitting down to prevent you falling or fainting or losing control of yourself *Are you sitting down?* Okay I will continue.)

I turned in my topic of choice for my thousand-word research paper as follows:

NAME: Houston Gunn

TOPIC: 1st Trust Deed Lending

The teacher called me over and told me, "No, you cannot do that topic."

"What! Why not?" I asked.

My teacher then replied, "There isn't a way to fill a thousand words that are required on this research paper for that topic. That topic would be too difficult to research. You will not be able to find enough information on that topic, on the computers, when we use them in the library for this project."

I told my teacher that I knew exactly where to find the research on that topic and that I knew enough about it already. I could fill a paper with more than a thousand words about first-trust deed lending. I told my teacher I was writing a book about this right now and had lent money in this manner personally. I tried to plead my case but was still firmly told no.

I was just fuming mad and could not wait to go home and tell my mom about this class assignment. I was so passionate about this that I made a decision right then and there that for all the class time over the next few weeks that the rest of the students worked on their research paper of a thousand words or more on their topic of choice, I was going to work on my book, which would be well over a thousand words and get me a lot further in life then this dumb paper.

*And I did just that.*

And the more I was fuming about this paper and getting just so angry about the injustice that had taken place in this classroom, the more motivated I got to finish my book and put this story in it. I guess I should have picked a more mainstream topic like *football, pizza,* or *trucks.*

When my teacher found I was not doing the research paper, and was writing this book instead, she told me to pick a topic of choice, and I replied that I already had and it had been rejected.

She then told me that if I did not pick a new topic by the next day that I would be assigned one. That night, I did not pick a different topic; instead, I started this chapter of my book and wrote about this incident instead.

The next day at school, I was humiliated and embarrassed when my teacher picked a topic and assigned it to me. My teacher told me my thousand-word research paper topic was going to be "Advertising toward Males."

I went home and told my family the topic she selected, and we all laughed and laughed as we imagined the thousand words that could be written about the Super Bowl beer commercials, the Little Blue Pill commercials (my uncle gave me that one). How about the Marlboro man and some Playboy ads as well? What the heck.

I slammed my paper out in about an hour. It was supposed to take weeks. I did not get a good grade on it; what can I say? My head was not in the game. My ideas were squashed and my motivation and enthusiasm towards this assignment was defeated. I had just experienced my first experience with a teacher where I appeared to be too square for the round-peg-hole class. I promised myself on that day that when this book is completed, I would mail my teacher an autographed copy so she could see that I am capable of writing a thousand words or more about topics that interest me. I hope my teacher reads it and understands that when you read, you achieve. I learned that in the first grade when I was in a series of public service announcement commercials with Ray Allen and the Seattle Supersonics for their reading and literacy campaign. At the end of the commercials, we all looked in the camera and shouted, "When you read, you achieve!"

I am not going to go into detail about the book that I was assigned to read in the same English class along with the research paper. My mom took it away and swapped books with me and my grandmother on a flight one day. Grandma Linda started reading it while I was working on other homework and came to a page where the boy was questioning if the animals in the zoo have sexual relations and they are animal siblings, is it incest or just sex? My grandma said, "Is this the best book they can find to assign to read?"

My mom challenged the teacher, the principal, and the school on that one, and she lost too. The time for a change was a coming. My mom had challenged the school several times before when my brother would report to her what was going on in his classrooms. The school said the solution was just to move us to other classes, as they could not do anything about the teachers because of their contracts. I think there might have been more to her moving idea than she let on.

Why can't we read books in classes that are going to benefit us later in life and teach us things we need to know? Maybe someday this book or a future book can be used to educate classes of teens on goal-setting and entrepreneurship. That would be *awesome*!

I hope this message helps teachers everywhere to encourage their square-peg students and motivate them, as you never know which ones will make a difference someday in the lives of somebody else. Teachers, please do not force-feed them topics they are uninspired to write about and make them read books that are not worth their time. Please give students work to take to make up when they will be out of school for the day—give them the work, *please*. And when they go on a family vacation for spring break during the week school is out, don't kick them off the sports team for missing three practices that week.

That is what my track coach did when I told him the day before spring break that I was going to Mexico with my family and would miss the three practices scheduled that week. I had been on the track team for almost a month and practiced every day, rain or shine. Mostly rain. My mom had just bought me new track shoes.

My track coach replied, "Well, I guess today's your last team practice for the season then."

I was stunned. That was the day I hung up my track shoes for good. And I liked track and was a fast runner. Well, I did not actually hang up my shoes; my mom went to the school office and set them very hard on the counter. She then gave them to the principal, asking him to please donate them to a free- or reduced-lunch student, who might need seventy-five-dollar track shoes and was not getting to go on a family vacation to Mexico over spring break.

He took the shoes.

What started as such a year of excitement was turning into a real disappointment. I guess I was getting older and starting to see things in a different light and have opinions of what is fair and just and right.

I flew out two days later to Mexico and took all the notebooks to work on this book and kissed the track team goodbye, so to speak. I guess you cannot do sports if you go on family vacations during the school closure for vacation weeks.

Yes, it was time for a change.

My mom got tickets May 3–10 for us to go to Nashville and look at houses. When there, I liked what I saw and whom I met, and I felt it had an atmosphere I could be around, not only with my music, but my life!

After a family discussion, we decided to make an offer on a house just outside of Nashville on sixteen acres, where my brother got his motorcycle track and a pond to fish in. I was only thirty minutes from Music City, USA, and would get to focus on my passion—*music*—and this book. We did not even wait for school to get out. My mom bought a house in three weeks, and we loaded up and drove caravan all the way across the country to our new home.

My grades were all fine in my other classes, except for Honors English. Whatever. I have never had an F before, and there is always a first for everything.

I only had a four-and-a-half-week summer break, as schools in Tennessee start the first of August. I started a new school and, best of all, get to work with music professionals, artists, and songwriters almost every night of the week after school. I even joined the Nashville Youth Symphony program.

As I'm the putting the finishing touches on this book, I am finishing my sophomore year at my new high school in Tennessee. Moving to Nashville has made me realize that I would like to be in the music business someday. I will work hard to be an artist, a musician, or a songwriter. That means it is time to set another goal.

I am continuing to work on my networking and am getting more comfortable every day. Just a few months ago, we were at Symphony Hall going to see the Chieftains perform, as my fiddle and mandolin instructor was touring with them across the United States. We had front-row seats for the show, and she brought us backstage afterward. Before the show began, I looked to my right, and there was Trace Adkins, the country music star, sitting three seats from me. After telling my mom, she challenged me—betting me twenty bucks—to go introduce myself to him. She said that it would be good for me. So I got out of my chair and walked on over to his seat and introduced myself, shook his hand, and told him what a fan I was and that I had seen him perform at the Grand Ole Opry last summer when we first moved here. He and I visited for another minute, and he thanked me for coming to talk to him. That was a great learning experience for me. I got to meet Trace Adkins and talk with him for a few minutes. I am a fan and can only hope to work with him someday. I was cheering him on during Donald Trump's *All-Star Celebrity Apprentice*, which he'd just won as well. I understand now on a much larger scale the power of networking and just how important it is.

Besides meeting the Chieftains, I have met several country music artists and celebrities backstage at the Grand Ole Opry, including Blake Shelton. Each time it becomes more and more comfortable for me to talk to them, as they are just people doing their jobs too.

Networking and the power of it! I have learned to always do it and never underestimate it, especially now.

~♮~

I hope my story has given you at least one ah-ha moment. If it did, then I did my job of sharing my message. Thank you for reading my opinions, views, thoughts, and experiences in life so far. I hope there are more books to come and that you read them too.

I invite you to join me or contact me via the following avenues:

Email me at: www.HoustonGunn.com

Twitter: @HoustonGunn

Facebook: Houston Gunn

To book an interview or a speaking engagement please contact me at www.HoustonGunn.com

If there is only one thing for you to remember after reading this book it is this:

> *When you work for others, you make them rich; when you work for yourself, you make yourself rich.*

Make goals-Date goals and take action.

Welcome change and challenge.

Thank you again for purchasing this book
and supporting an entrepreneur.

I am one step closer to my goal of purchasing a blue
Corvette while I am still sixteen years old.

# What are your next goals?

| Goal | Date |
| --- | --- |
| | |
| | |
| | |
| | |
| | |
| | |
| | |
| | |
| | |
| | |
| | |
| | |
| | |
| | |
| | |
| | |
| | |

CPSIA information can be obtained at www.ICGtesting.com
Printed in the USA
BVOW08s1136301013

335036BV00001B/16/P